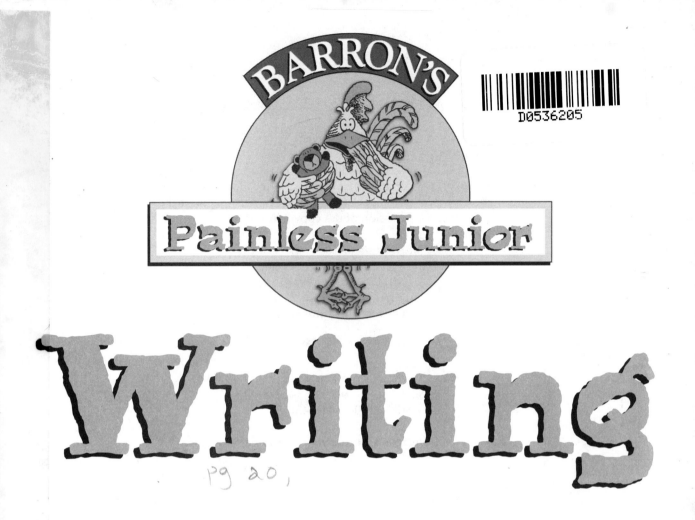

BARRON'S

Painless Junior

Writing

pg 20,

Donna Christina Oliverio, M.S.

BARRON'S

All inquiries should be addressed to:
Barron's Educational Series, Inc.
250 Wireless Boulevard
Hauppauge, New York 11788
www.barronseduc.com

Library of Congress Control Number: 2006045989
ISBN-13: 978-0-7641-3438-8
ISBN-10: 0-7641-3438-8

Library of Congress Cataloging-in-Publication Data

Oliverio, Donna Christina.
    Painless junior, writing / Donna Christina Oliverio.
        p.   cm.
    Includes index.
    ISBN-13: 978-0-7641-3438-8
    ISBN-10: 0-7641-3438-8
    1. English language—Composition and exercises—Juvenile literature. 2. English language—Composition and exercises—Study and teaching (Elementary)—Juvenile literature. 3. Creative writing (Elementary education)—Juvenile literature. I. Title.

PE1408.O44   2006
372.62'3—dc22   2006045989

PRINTED IN THE UNITED STATES OF AMERICA
9 8 7 6 5 4 3 2 1

Dedication

This book is for Kids
who want to have as much fun writing
as a dolphin playfully skimming the waves
and
for Mom, Rocco, and Jay Jay

Acknowledgments

I am grateful to my family. To Mom, for filling my childhood with the three L's: love, literature, and lasagna. To Uncle John, for adding the fourth L: laughter. And to Jay, for letting me see the world through the eyes of an artist and nature enthusiast.

I also wish to acknowledge Vivian, Ming, Anthony, Jimmy, Brandon, Mun, Yeng, and Larry . . . and the folks at Barron's, especially Pat Hunter, Bob O'Sullivan, Wayne Barr, Veronica Douglas, and the Art and Production Department.

Last, but not least, I am grateful to Josh for giving me constructive feedback on my manuscript. Josh, if you never hear another simile, I'm sure you'll be as happy as a clownfish riding the current into open waters.

Contents

Introduction: Oceans of Fun for Everyone!

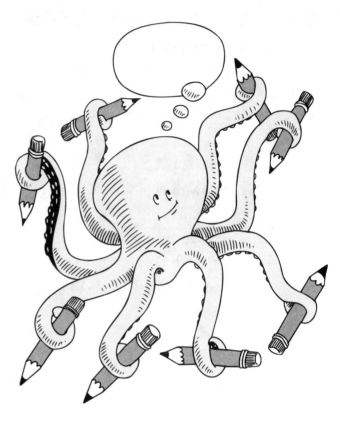

MEET SAMMY, THE WRITING OCTOPUS

Hi, Authors and Captains!

I'm an octopus who loves to write. Trust me! I didn't always feel that way.

While growing up in the Pacific Ocean, I spent most of my time watching TV, playing video games, and hanging out at the Starfish Mall. Then, one calm night at sea, I climbed on board the fun ship, Authorship. My life has not been the same since.

These days, my brain is churning with ideas for writing. Luckily, I have eight arms and enough ink to put all my ideas on paper or on computer screen. I'm also lucky to have a large brain because thinking and writing are like peanut butter and jelly—they really go together.

Earlier today, I wrote a newspaper article about a real happening in my life. What I'm about to tell you may sound fishy, but it's true.

For the past month, a school of misbehaving fish has been playing hide-and-seek outside my cave and keeping me from getting my beauty sleep. It is hard to build muscles and make ink for writing when I don't get enough rest.

Tomorrow, I'm going to write a poem and comic strip about a shipwreck on a desert island. Writing is painless! You can take one idea and write a gazillion pieces about it.

Wow! Yippee! Now, it's time to live out the adventures of an octopus who loves writing (that's me!), a green sea turtle who is searching for treasure, an unusual chicken who points out big ideas on your journey, and other amazing water creatures and wildlife. Off we sail, surf, swim, dive, splash, drift, float, row, paddle, plunge, explore . . . and a whole lot more!

Big Smiles and Waves,

Sammy, the Writing Octopus
(also called Sammy Octopus or Sammy, for short)

UNDERWATER BOOKSTORE: ABOUT *PAINLESS JUNIOR WRITING*

Painless Junior Writing takes you on an exciting journey into the A-B-Seas of Writing. As soon as your adventure gets underway, the feel of the cool ocean water will wake you up, and you will begin to notice the small wonders around you. A few sea miles later, you will learn how to turn those small wonders into writing treasures that will thrill readers from coast to coast.

On your painless journey, there are no rules for writing, only coaching tips. As the captain of your own ship, you get to pick and choose the writing moves that work best for you. Now that's painless, but not brainless, writing!

Leave your troubles ashore. Get ready for fun and surprises. Put on your goggles and dive right in like a dolphin!

BEST-KEPT SECRET OF THE DEEP

Pssst . . . Do you want to know the best-kept secret of the sea? (Come close.)

Great writers are not superheroes with special powers: They're kids and people like YOU. Pssst . . . Do you want to solve the mystery behind how a water creature becomes friends with a land animal? Well, you've come to the right place. You've come to the Friendship Dock!

Sammy Octopus and Scuba Susie met each other for the first time through a group of creatures and wildlife they have in common. You see . . . Sammy is friends with a green sea turtle named Tammy, who just so happens to have a land turtle named Tierra for a cousin, and Tierra is friends with Scuba Susie, the chicken.

When Scuba Susie saw Sammy Octopus for the first time, the puff of feathers on her head stood straight up. She was amazed that he had eight arms and that he could make ink. In turn, Sammy Octopus was amazed by Scuba Susie's beak, feathers, and weird-looking feet. (Her toes are as long as the open sea.) And so began the tale of tentacles and feathers, of sea and land, of strangers and friends.

Icon Key

Let's Try It!
A quiz to practice what
you have learned.

Key Points!
Important ideas that you
should keep in mind.

Careful!
Problems you might
come across.

Wrapping It Up!
A summary of key ideas.

Chapter I

Set Sail with Talking Marine Animals

TAMMY TURTLE FEELS LIKE A FISH OUT OF WATER

CHARACTERS:

Octopus: A giant Pacific octopus named Sammy, the Writing Octopus.

Turtle: A green sea turtle named Tammy, the Thinking Turtle (She swims to the surface to breathe every few minutes.)

SETTING: Underwater Kingdom in the Pacific Ocean.

ATTENTION ALL READERS: HOLD YOUR BREATH. WE'RE GOING UNDER!

Octopus: What are you doing on this lovely summer night, Tammy?

Turtle: I'm trying to write a story, but it's hard to get started. When there is a blank piece of paper in front of me, I feel like a school bus stuck in mud or snow.

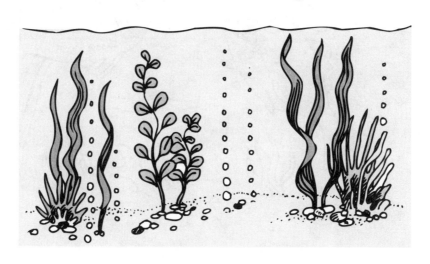

Octopus: Sometimes I have the same problem, and I'm sure other authors do, too.

Turtle: What should I do when my imagination is on vacation, and I don't know what to write?

Octopus: Fish around for ideas. They are all around you. Some are big and easy to see. Others are small and hidden. Be on the lookout for those ideas that mean the most to you—ones you really care about, including those stored in your memory.

Turtle: I CARE that I'm a member of an endangered species. Wow! I could write a million different pieces about that one idea: Saving Sea Turtles. From now on, I will observe my world closely.

Octopus: Carry a notebook and pencil with you so you can jot down ideas the moment they pop into your head. You can look back at your notebook whenever you are staring at a blank sheet of paper and need ideas to write about.

Turtle: The Starfish Mall has these really cool note pads with boogie boards on them. I'll swim over there tomorrow and buy one. See you later, alligator. Oops, I mean see you later, octopus.

Octopus: After a while, crocodile. I mean after a while, green sea turtle.

OBSERVATION ISLAND: SEE A SEA OF SEED IDEAS GROW

Has either of these things ever happened to you? You get to school and realize that you left your lunch or homework at home. Or, you go to write something and find that your pencil needs sharpening.

Here's why I ask. The little happenings, or small moments, in your everyday life can grow into huge writing treasures. Let's say, for example, you decide to write a story about your pencil. As a writer, you have a scientist's mind. You wonder, "Where does my pencil point go?" As a writer, you also have an artist's eye. So, you might start out writing about a missing pencil point, but end up writing a more exciting story about life in a classroom— you know, all the stuff that students deal with during the school day.

Here's the point about the pointless pencil piece. Good writers like you can take a little idea and turn it into something BIG.

Writing is not about finding topics that are larger than life. You can write about anyone or anything in your life that matters to you— like your parents, playground, or puppy . . . or your friendships, French fries, or Frisbees.

Whatever your favorite topic or idea is, try writing different kinds of pieces about it, such as a poem, short story, picture book, journal entry, report, essay, newspaper article, A-B-C book, letter, song, and comic strip. Soon, you'll be saying, "There aren't enough months in the year, weeks in the month, days in the week, hours in the day, or seconds in the minute to write all that I want to write."

Key Points!

In some ways, writers are like scientists. They observe the world around them and ask a lot of questions. Often they jot down notes about their findings.

In many ways, writers are like artists. They keep their artists' eyes wide open, and notice the little happenings or goings-on in their lives.

Good writers turn small ideas into big writing treasures.

Let's Try It!

Set #1

Look at the world around you. Write down eight ideas from your own life that you care about. Each time you think of another idea, add it to your list. Your list does not have to be written using complete sentences.

 Happy Hint: Try looking back at this list whenever you feel stuck and don't know what to write next.

ALL ABOARD THE FUN SHIP, *AUTHORSHIP*

CHARACTERS:

Narrator

Turtle: A green sea turtle named Tammy, the Thinking Turtle

Cuttlefish: A cuttlefish named Carlos

Octopus: A giant Pacific octopus named Sammy, the Writing Octopus

SETTING: The Pacific coast of North America

Narrator: Tammy, the Thinking Turtle, looked as though she was crying, so her friend Carlos asked her what was wrong.

Turtle: I'm not crying. I'm just trying to get rid of all the salty seawater that my body soaks up every day.

Narrator: Carlos was glad to hear that Tammy was okay.

Cuttlefish: I think you should write a story about your special tears or about how you know to return to the same beach where you were born to lay your eggs. Kids would find it amazing.

Turtle: I am not good at writing.

Narrator: Just then Sammy, the Writing Octopus, appeared. He overheard what Tammy had said about herself.

Sammy looked down, his arms dropped to the sea floor, and his skin coloring changed. Sensing Sammy's sadness, Carlos decided to swim off and leave his friends alone to talk. (The sounds of Carlos swimming swiftly away are heard in the background: Splash! Splosh!)

Octopus: Tammy, think of writing as playing a video game. When you are first learning how to play a new game, you may not know the best moves to make. Then, over time, you become better with practice.

Turtle: I'm good at playing video games because I practice. Soon, I'll also be gr-r-reat at playing the writing game, because I'll spend more time reading, writing, and thinking.

Octopus: [clapping his eight arms] Way to go, Tammy! Yes, writing, reading, and thinking are like peas in a pod. They're all closely connected.

Turtle: By reading a lot and by reading different types of writing (fiction, nonfiction, and poetry), I can see how authors play with words, language, and ideas. Other writers, then, are like my teachers and coaches.

Octopus: Y-e-s-s-s! Try to read every piece that you can get your flippers on. Your favorite authors can help you get ready for the A-B-Seas of Writing, so you won't be lost at sea or give up the great ship: *Authorship*.

Narrator: At that moment, Sammy began squirting black ink. Tammy thought he was getting ready to write something down, until she spotted a shark lurking nearby. Lucky for Sammy and Tammy, the dark-colored ink clouded the water, making it hard for the predator to spot his prey. The two friends escaped without losing a tentacle or flipper.

This whirlwind of activity made the octopus and turtle hungry. Sammy pounced on a crab and devoured his dinner on the sea floor. Tammy, a herbivore (plant eater), chomped on flowering plants in the sea.

Then suddenly, a group of scuba divers invaded Sammy and Tammy's space. The two sea creatures, annoyed at all the goings-on, decided to call it a night.

Let's Try It!

Set #2

1. Sammy helped Tammy learn about writing. What did you learn about writing from Sammy?

2. How will you use what you learned to improve your writing?

3. Ask one or two people to read aloud with you the dialogues about writing that take place on pages 3–5 and 8–11. Take turns playing the parts of the octopus, turtle, narrator, and cuttlefish. Think about making costumes for the characters. Perform the play for an audience, such as your classmates, friends, or family members. Use your best acting skills!

LIFESAVING TIPS ON WRITING

✔ **Have fun with writing**

- Don't tell yourself you can't write. Think about all the things you can do well as an author. Think of writing as playing with words.

- You have something BIG to say. Write about ideas that are important to you. Share your writing with readers.

Write every day

- Practice your writing. Try writing different pieces such as thank-you notes, free writes, e-mails/instant messages, poems, short stories, journal entries, reports, recipes, picture books, lists, songs, and newspaper articles.

Read, read some more, and reread

- Good writers are good readers.
- Read as much as you can and read different types of written works: poetry, nonfiction, and fiction.
- Slow down and reread important details.

Learn from other writers

- You can learn from other writers, including your classmates.
- Try to figure out how a piece is written. As you are reading or rereading, ask yourself questions such as: "Why did the writer begin or end a story this way?" "What special effect is the author trying to create for readers here?" "How did the poet choose 'just-right' words?" The answers to these questions may give you ideas for improving your writing.

Celebrate

- Kick up your heels, and go dance with the seals. Make a big deal. You are an author!

Wrapping It Up!

Ideas for writing can be found anywhere between the bottom of the sea and the top of the clouds.

Good writers like you observe the world closely. They look up and down, over and around, here and there. By doing so, they come up with ideas that they can develop into writing pieces.

Chapter 2

Getting Your Feet Wet for the A-B-Seas of Writing

In Chapter 1, we swam alongside talking sea animals and learned that ideas for writing are all around us. In this chapter, we'll ride on Sammy Octopus's tentacles and discover different ways to rehearse, or plan, for writing.

Writers believe what they have to say is important, and they want their readers to believe it is, too. From beginning to end, authors like you keep in mind WHY they are writing and FOR WHOM they are writing.

AN OCEAN OF REASONS: PURPOSE

There are many purposes, or reasons, for writing. Here are a few. You can write to:

- ✔ **tell a story**

- ✔ **entertain readers**

- ✔ **describe a special memory or place**

- ✔ **teach something (like how to build a sandcastle)**

- ✔ **explore ideas or feelings**

Sammy Octopus and Tammy Turtle have their own purposes for writing. Sammy's main reason for putting his thoughts on paper is to show readers that writing is painless and fun. Tammy Turtle writes to convince readers to help save sea turtles. Both of these sea animals write from their hearts; they have a need to tell their stories.

Before putting your thoughts down on paper, ask yourself, "*Why* am I writing?" Keep your purposes for writing in mind the whole time that you're putting your ideas onto the written page. If you care about your reasons for writing, readers will care about what you have to say.

A SEA OF READERS: AUDIENCE

Just as there are many reasons for writing, there are many types of readers. Your audience can include friends, family, classmates, teachers, the entire school body, your local community, and the federal government. Your audience always includes yourself.

It helps to know who your readers are because it can change the way you write. For example, you might scribble a note to your dad, but you wouldn't scribble one to the president of the United States.

Sammy Octopus keeps his readers in mind the whole time he is writing—from the moment he has an idea in his head to the time he has a finished piece in his tentacles. His audience is made up of kids who are in elementary or middle school . . . and himself. Sammy writes to please himself; he wants "who he is" to come shining through the pages.

UNDER THE DEEP BLUE WITH YOU: VOICE

Once you have a purpose and an audience that you care about, your voice will stand out like Dorothy's ruby slippers in *The Wizard of Oz.*

You know about voice. It's your personal stamp, or fingerprint on writing. It lets the reader know that YOU, a real person, are behind the written words.

Careful!

Writing is not about using fancy words that sound as though a computer, robot, or someone else put them on the page. If you want to connect with readers, YOU must be present in your piece. Your voice must be heard.

Reread the Introduction of this book on page viii, and try to listen for Sammy's voice. Even though you have never met Sammy, I'll bet you can get a sense of what he's like through his word choices. Many readers think that Sammy is one cool cat . . . I mean one cool octopus. His voice makes readers giggle. He uses everyday words well.

Like other writers, Sammy changes his voice depending on his purpose for writing and his audience. For example, when Sammy is writing about all the pollution at sea, his voice makes readers feel how he feels: mad, sad, scared, discouraged, and disappointed.

You have power as a writer. Once you have a topic you love and readers you care about, your voice will jump off the pages and stay in the reader's mind for ages!

Key Points!

If you want your voice to come shining through the pages like the sun after a storm at sea, keep the focus on *why* and *for whom* you are writing. When you have a purpose and audience you care about, readers see you as a real person speaking to them, and they care about what you have to say.

DO WHAT WORKS FOR YOU, CAPTAIN

Writers pick and choose the moves that work best for them and for the pieces they are writing. Sometimes, they run with the ideas they have in their heads and begin writing rough drafts right away. Other times, they think their ideas through before putting them on paper.

Think of each piece you write as a new adventure. When you go on an adventure for the first time, you probably have some idea of where you're going and what you'll be doing. Yet, you won't know exactly how your adventure will turn out—until you've gone on it. Likewise, writers often do not know exactly what they will write or how pieces will turn out—until they've completed their writing adventures.

WRITING A REPORT

Let's say that you've decided to write a report on octopuses. The reason you are writing is to inform (tell) your readers about these smart sea creatures. Your audience is made up of kids between the ages of eight and twelve, and yourself of course. What will you do to get yourself ready to write?

The octopus drawing and the rest of this chapter explain what you can do to gather ideas for writing and to rethink your ideas, as needed, during writing.

In the Swim of Things: Gathering Ideas

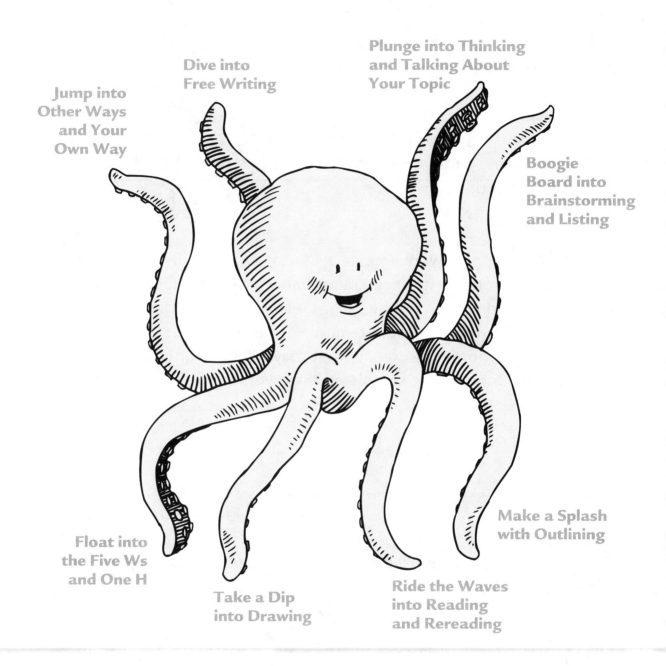

Jump into
Other Ways
and Your
Own Way

Dive into
Free Writing

Plunge into Thinking
and Talking About
Your Topic

Boogie
Board into
Brainstorming
and Listing

Float into
the Five Ws
and One H

Take a Dip
into Drawing

Ride the Waves
into Reading
and Rereading

Make a Splash
with Outlining

DIVE INTO FREE WRITING

When you free write, you are talking to yourself on paper (or on computer screen). Free writing can help you get started.

Here is one way to go about free writing. Set aside a short amount of time (about five or ten minutes). Write down all the thoughts that come into your head as quickly as you can. Don't worry about spelling, grammar, or punctuation.

Write for the whole time even if you must write "Blah, blah, blah" or "I don't know what to write next," until you think of something else. Soon, ideas will start to fizz around your brain; and abracadabra! You will get back on track. Stop free writing when your time is up.

Let's look at an example.

Sample Free Write for Report Writing

Today we studied sea creatures in class. We are going to do reports on see life. I chose an octopus to write about. Why an octopus. I don't know really. I know I have a soccer game tonite. I know its an invertebrate and so is a butterfly. Invertebrates have no back bones. A octopus has 8 arms, it's like having arms without bones. Octopus gives off ink to scare away moray eel. They're like dolphins—learn thru mimicry. I don't know what to write next. Octopus are smart they can open lids on jars and solve mazes. Blah, blah I don't now what to write. They escape from aquarims like magician. Their artists all right, escape artists. One octopus that escaped ended up in library flipping thru pages of a book (true story). Aquarium keepers need to put xtra protection in tanks so octopus won't get out.

Notice that in the first few sentences of the free write, the writer is not saying much of anything. Then the words and sentences come alive, once the writer begins adding important details to the passage. Also, although there are spelling and grammar errors in the free write, they do not stop readers from understanding what the writer is trying to say.

Let's Try It!

Take five minutes to write freely about an octopus or a sea creature of your choice. On your mark . . . get set . . . free write!

When you're done free writing, reread what you have written and underline ideas you could use in your report on octopuses.

PLUNGE INTO THINKING AND
TALKING ABOUT YOUR TOPIC

Would you believe it if I told you that Sammy Octopus thinks about his writing while he's doing chores? (Well, he does!) Sammy tries to come up with details and a direction for his paper when he's doing boring jobs, like picking teeny-tiny pieces of shell off his bedroom floor. As for Tammy Turtle, she shares her ideas with other water creatures before she writes them down.

Ideas for writing can pop into your head at any time and place (on the playground, at a friend's house, in the movie theater). Try to keep a notepad and pencil with you at all times so you can jot down ideas as you think of them.

Careful!

Before putting your ideas into sentences and paragraphs, you might find it helpful to rehearse what you want to say and how you want to say it.

As you're thinking and talking about your topic, try to imagine how your piece will grow over time—and, how it will grow on your readers.

Let's Try It!

Spend time thinking through the details of your report on octopuses. Then ask someone like a classmate or family member to listen to you as you are talking and to give you suggestions or advice.

23

Boogie Board into Brainstorming and Listing

When you brainstorm, you are trying to come up with as many ideas that relate to your topic as possible.

Think about what you already know about your topic. Look up information you don't know. List your ideas and the facts you've learned using words or short phrases, rather than complete sentences.

Example

Octopuses:

Most live alone

Change colors to hide from predators & camouflage themselves

Eat crab & other shellfish; also eat dead animals (scavengers)

_____

_____

_____

_____

_____

Let's Try It!

Add five more facts about octopuses to the list above. Read some books on octopuses or search the Internet for additional facts if you need help.

MAKE A SPLASH WITH OUTLINING

Sometimes, it is helpful to outline your ideas before writing. An outline is like a list, but it is usually more organized. It helps you see how ideas are connected or related.

Here's a sample outline on the topic of octopuses.

Topic: Octopuses

I. Introduction

II. Octopuses Should Rule the Sea

   A. Smart

   B. Can solve problems

   C. Good memories

   D. Like dolphins, octopuses learn from each other (mimicry)

III. Body Parts

    A. Eight rubbery arms

    B. Soft body

    C. No bones

    D. _____

    E. _____

IV. Fun Facts About Octopuses

    A. Big eaters

    B. Squirt ink to chase away moray eels

    C. _____

    D. _____

    E. _____

V. Female Octopuses

    A. Thousands of eggs

    B. _____

    C. _____

VI. Conclusion

Let's Try It!

Complete the outline. Use the library or Internet to help you. (Note: Many answers are possible.)

Ride the Waves into Reading and Rereading

Read as much as you can about octopuses. Use the library and Internet to help you with your research. Take breaks from your reading, and talk about what you've read with someone like a classmate. If possible, interview an expert on sea life, like a marine biologist (scientist).

When you find something helpful or interesting in your reading, slow down and take the time to give it another look. As you are rereading, ask yourself, "What is it about this writing that makes it good or that makes it stand out?" The answer to this question might give you clues for improving your own writing.

Take notes on the main or BIG ideas that you come across in your reading and also on your feelings about what you're reading. Think about how you might organize (group together neatly) all your ideas and information.

Careful!

To do a research project, you need *facts* (information that is *true*). Yet, it's up to YOU as the writer to make sense of the facts you come across in your reading. It's up to YOU to explore the facts, to dig deeply into them like a dog searching for a buried bone, to think about and question them, and to write about them in a way that shows readers you've come up with your own understanding of the research topic.

Let's Try It!

Begin your research project on octopuses. Read and reread as many books and magazine articles as you can. You may also use the Internet. Talk about what you are reading with other people, as often as you can. Take notes on the BIG ideas in your reading, and also on your thoughts about what you are reading. You will use these notes later on, when it comes time to write a rough draft of your report. Happy Researching!

TAKE A DIP INTO DRAWING

Sometimes, drawing can wake up our imagination and help us get ideas for writing, as well as help us learn (see) a topic better. Other times, it can distract us and take time away from our writing.

If you choose to draw before writing, it may help to set aside a short period of time (about five or ten minutes) to do so. After your time is up, stop drawing and begin writing. You can always go back to drawing later, once you see how your paper is coming along.

Let's Try It!

Draw your own octopus and label its body parts: arms, suckers, mouth, eyes, mantle, and funnel. If you need help, look at drawings of octopuses in books and magazines or on the Internet.

FLOAT INTO THE FIVE WS AND ONE H

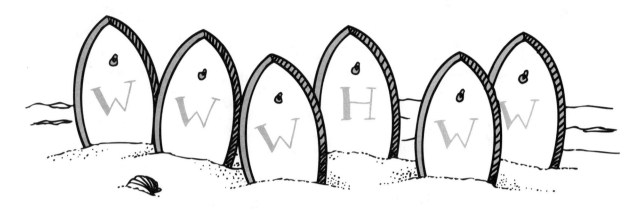

Newspaper reporters often use the five Ws and one H to gather a lot of information about a topic quickly. You know about the five W's and one H: Who, What, Where, When, Why, and How. You can use these questions to explore your topic.

Example
Who: Octopuses
What: A nonfiction report on octopuses

Let's Try It!

Answer the rest of the five Ws and one H questions. Use the library or Internet if you need help.

Where: (Where do octopuses live? In what parts of the world are they found?)

_____

When: (Are you writing about a special time period? Will you need to give your readers dates that relate to your topic? If not, you may leave this answer blank.)

_____

Why: (Why are you writing about this topic? Why is it important?)

_____

How: (How will you go about writing your report?)

_____

JUMP INTO OTHER WAYS AND YOUR OWN WAY

There are other moves you can make to get ready to write. Here are a few:

✔ **Create a graphic organizer such as a word web or timeline**

✔ **Listen to music**

✔ **Watch a movie**

✔ **Come up with your own way**

I wonder how you will prepare for writing. Maybe you'll use some of the ideas in this chapter. Maybe you'll come up with ones of your own. Let's jump into the next activity and find out.

Let's Try It!

Come up with your own way to plan or rehearse for writing a report. It doesn't have to be anything big or fancy; it just has to work for you. Share your plan with other writers.

Happy Hint: If you have trouble inventing a new way and would rather use one of the ways we talked about earlier, feel free to do so. Sammy Octopus promised you this book was going to be painless, and Sammy always keeps his promises.

Wrapping It Up!

If you want your writing to sound like YOU wrote it, keep your reasons for writing and your readers in mind the whole time.

Writers rehearse or plan for writing in different ways. Sometimes, they dive right in and don't plan at all. Other times, they get their feet wet before they write. Some of the more common ways to plan for writing include thinking and talking about the topic, free writing, brainstorming and listing, outlining, and reading.

Writing is painless: As an author, you get to pick and choose the moves that work best for YOU and for the piece you are writing.

Let's Try It!

Set #3

Using the library and/or Internet, research the differences between a sea turtle and a turtle. Some differences to look for include the animal's habitat, diet (food), and nesting habits—and any others you might come across in your reading. While researching, notice also how a sea turtle and a turtle are alike. Write a summary or short report about your findings.

Happy Hint: Before writing, you may want to collect and organize your thoughts using a Venn diagram, such as the one shown below. Or, feel free to use any of the ways you've learned in this chapter to plan for writing.

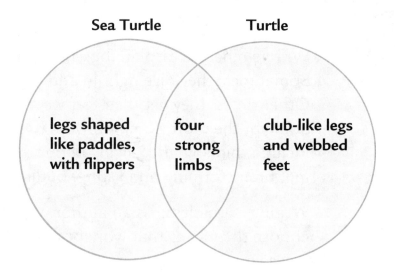

Sea Turtle   Turtle

legs shaped like paddles, with flippers   four strong limbs   club-like legs and webbed feet

Chapter 3

Rough Draft
Writing and Revising

FEEL THE FREEDOM OF THE OPEN OCEAN: WRITE A ROUGH DRAFT

So far, we've talked about gathering small ideas in our everyday lives and rehearsing them, as needed, before writing. Now, let's chat about writing a rough draft (copy).

A rough draft is the starting point where you begin to put your ideas into sentences and paragraphs. Sometimes, even when you've rehearsed for writing, the blank piece of paper staring back at you makes you feel seasick. Whatever you do, keep your chin *up* and do NOT give *up*.

Getting started is often the hardest part for many writers. When Sammy Octopus gets stuck and doesn't know how to begin his paper, he sets a goal for himself that he knows he can reach. His goal might be to write one page, or two paragraphs, or even one sentence—whatever he thinks he can get down on paper.

Shortly after reaching his goal, Sammy becomes un-stuck. He gets so many ideas that he wishes he had as many appendages as a cuttlefish to keep up with all the writing he wants to do. By setting a goal for yourself, you too will be bursting with ideas for writing. Maybe you'll wish you had as many arms as an octopus, to keep up with all the writing you want to do.

A rough draft gives you the freedom of the open ocean. It gives you the chance to focus on what you are trying to say, without worrying too much about spelling, capitalization, punctuation, and grammar. Still, you should try to write the draft as well as you can.

Later, when it comes time to revise and edit your work, you can rethink your ideas and correct any errors that may be in your draft. If you write on every other line of your draft, there will be extra space for you to make changes (like cut-and-paste sentences) and improve your work.

Careful!

A rough draft is sometimes called a sloppy copy. The rhyming name is easy to remember, but it can give you the wrong idea about rough draft writing.

Your rough draft or sloppy copy does not have to be perfect, but you should try to write it as *neatly* as you can and as well as you can.

SHARING BY THE SHORE: CELEBRATION

You don't have to wait until your paper is in perfect shape to share it with others. Sammy says, "Celebrate the author in you whenever and wherever you can." By reading aloud your rough draft to people you know and trust, you can get ideas for improving your work. Sammy shares his writing with others every chance he gets. Like you, Sammy is an author, and he is mighty proud of it.

Key Points!

Your goal in writing a rough draft is to get your ideas down on paper. Write the draft as well as you can, without worrying too much about rules. Share your rough draft, and celebrate the author in you whenever and wherever you can!

SAMMY OCTOPUS'S BEST FRIEND

Revising is one of Sammy Octopus's best friends, and he hopes it will become one of yours as well. *Revising* is another word for *seeing again*.

Here's how Sammy Octopus goes about revising, or seeing his writing again.

✔ **He rereads his rough draft many times.**

✔ **He rethinks his ideas.**

✔ **He makes changes, as needed, to improve his writing.**

37

Revising, then, is more than just copying a paper neatly. It involves thinking and rewriting.

grandmas ho~~~~ isn't too far

Now you know why revising is Sammy's best buddy. By giving his draft a second, third, and even fourth look, Sammy is able to make his writing clear and enjoyable to read. And, so can you!

SEASAW BETWEEN DRAFTING AND REVISING

Revising is not the last stop on your writing journey. Many writers *revise* their drafts as they go—as they are writing them. They spend time *sea*sawing between writing a rough

draft of their ideas and rereading and revising them. For example, they write one or two sentences, and then reread and revise what they've written.

The back-and-forth movement between drafting and revising continues until the rough draft is finished. Then, writers go back to the beginning and reread and revise the completed draft. They might also ask other people like teachers or friends to reread their work.

Key Points!

Writing a paper without rereading and revising it is like flying a kite with a short string. You can do it, but you won't get very far.

Revising does *not* mean that you as a writer have done something wrong. It means that you have done something right and are taking steps to make a good piece of writing even better.

Let's Try It!

Set #4

Using the ideas you've gathered in Chapter 2, write a rough draft of your report on octopuses. If you need more information on octopuses, do some more reading and researching.

Happy Hint: The sample outline on pages 25–26 gives you an idea of how you can organize, or set up, your draft.

THE ISLE OF POETRY

I'm sure you've heard nursery rhymes, songs, and TV ads that sound like poetry. But what exactly is a poem? Is it just a string of rhyming words?

Poetry is a special type of writing that is in a class by itself. Think of fiction as being in one class, nonfiction as being in another, and poetry in yet another. Poems do not have to rhyme, but some have a rhythm or special beat to them. Many of them sound as pretty as a songbird.

Poetry gives you the freedom to share your deepest feelings and your hidden thoughts—to say what you really want to say—without focusing too much on the rules of writing. Yet, this freedom does not mean that you should, or even would want to, litter your poem with a sea of errors.

Good poets like you do not break writing rules just for the sake of breaking them. If they break rules at all, poets do so for the overall good of their pieces. They know that too many errors can lead readers to stop reading. Good poets like you do not break many rules, because they want readers to enjoy and understand their feelings and their messages.

IDEAS FOR POETRY

You can get ideas for poetry topics in the same way that you get them for other kinds of writing: by looking around your world and asking questions. Try to keep a notebook with you at all times so that you can jot down ideas as soon as they come to you.

You can write a poem about any-thing that is important to you, from cartwheels and skis to favorite meals and bruised knees. Unless you go through life with your eyes, ears, and nose closed, ideas for poetry will always be all around you. Just look out your porthole or window; life is full of little wonders that you can write big poems about.

Careful!

If you want to write a poem about lollipops and cotton candy, for example, try to write about *how those things make you feel* and *how you want readers to understand your feelings.*

A poem that is written by a kid who loves lollipops and cotton candy will be different from one that is written by a dentist. In describing your topic, try to give readers details they can see, hear, taste, smell, and feel—like *rainbow-colored, fluffy, candy clouds on a stick that make you feel like floating.*

Many poems are written about the environment (your surroundings). Poets just like you notice the little wonders that happen in nature, like squirrels arguing over an acorn or farmers growing corn from seeds. Then, if an idea or activity is special to them—if it tugs at their hearts— they write about it.

Good poets are able to make readers see, hear, and feel what they feel. Can't you just picture those two squirrels playing tug-of-war with that tasty acorn?

"It's MY acorn!" "No, it's not." "Mom, Chomper is not being fair; he's hogging all the food."

WRITING AND REVISING POEMS

Do you know what time it is? Cool beans, Captain. It's time for a poem!

Green

Green, Green, Green
I like GREEN!
A better color
I have
never
ever
seen.
It makes me want to scream,
Nature, Nature, Nature!

So, what do you think about the poem? Do you think it is packed to the gills with details? Keep in mind that it's a first draft.

Here's what Sammy Octopus says about "Green."

"Vrrooom! The poem 'Green' is off to a good start. It has a catchy rhyme and beat, and it does show the poet's love of the topic.

"'Green' is not perfect, but as a draft, it doesn't have to be. During revising, the poet might focus on adding details to the poem that readers can see, such as a baby otter wrapped in *seaweed*."

After listening to what Sammy said about "Green," the poet spent time brainstorming and listing ideas before revising the draft of the poem.

Example
Brainstorming and Listing Ideas for Poetry Writing

Topic: The Color Green
- greatest color of all
- color of nature
- trees, frog, lily pad
- leaves, grass, spinach, peas
- my favorite color

Here is a revised version of the poem.

REVISED DRAFT: RHYMING POETRY

Green

Green is the grass swaying in the wind.
Green are the leaves of a tree.
Green is nature's pretty color.
Green is a birthstone to me.
Green is spinach, cabbage, and lettuce.
Green covers the corn.
Green is a plump, juicy grape.
Green is an apple when born.
Green is the color with the special touch.
Green is different from all the rest!
Green is the color I like very much.
Green is the color that fits me best!

I'll bet the revised poem helps you see a picture of the color green in your mind. Perhaps you can see the grass swaying in the wind and maybe even feel the passing breeze. And, don't forget that plump, juicy grape. Yummy!

In the revised draft of "Green," the poet had to find rhyming words that also made sense in the poem. Writing (and reading) rhyming poetry can be fun, but sometimes it is tricky to say all that you want to say in a rhyme.

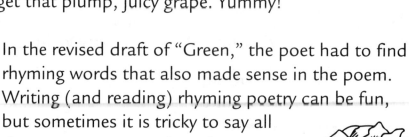

Revised Draft: Nonrhyming Poetry

The next poem, which is titled "Princess Green," uses ideas from "Green," but it does not use rhyme.

Princess Green

I skip through the park.
Stop, Smile.
There She is!
Looking pretty as a princess
my favorite color
all dressed up
in nature.
With eyes *evergreen,*
her crown, *moss* and *leaves.*

I skip through the park.
Stop, smile.
There She is!
The *emerald grass*
swaying gently in the wind.
A passing *frog*
hopping onto a *lily pad.*

I skip through the park.
Stop, smile.
There She is!
A *green-shelled turtle*
on a log, sunbathing.
A *largemouth bass*
jumping like a circus acrobat.

I skip home.
Stop, smile.
Thinking of her gifts.

The poet of "Princess Green" uses carefully chosen words and details, rather than rhyme, to create word pictures for readers. One such example can be found in the lines: "my favorite color / all dressed up / in nature." These just-right details show readers the close connection between the color green and nature.

The line breaks in poetry are important. Notice the description of the turtle in the poem: "A *green-shelled turtle* / on a log, sunbathing." By placing the word "sunbathing" at the end of a line in the poem, the poet gets readers to stop for a second, picture someone sunbathing (sunbathing is often connected with people, rather than animals), and then connect that picture of someone basking in the sun with a green-shelled turtle.

Imagine how different the poem would sound and read if the poet changed the order of a few words and then divided the lines as follows:

A *green-shelled turtle* sunbathing on a log.

Here, the word picture is not about a turtle sunbathing itself like a real person. It's more about a turtle that is resting on a log, rather than on a rock or dead tree stump, for example.

Poets often use a figure of speech called a simile to help readers see details in their poems. A simile compares unlike things using the word *like* or *as*. The lines "A *largemouth bass* / jumping like a circus acrobat" contain a simile: A fish and an acrobat are unlike things and the word *like* is used to compare them.

Reread the poem and see if you can figure out what the color green is being compared to. If you answered a princess, pat yourself on the back. The lines "Looking pretty as a princess / my favorite color" contain a simile because they use the word *as* to compare unlike things: a princess and the poet's favorite color (green).

A simile can be as helpful to your poem as a fireman is to a cat stuck in a tree (another simile). If you want to learn more about similes, float on over to Chapter 8.

A Treasure Trove of Tips

Here are some painless tips for writing poetry.

1. Read, listen to, and collect as many poems as possible. Let your favorite poets show you how to write powerful poetry. Or, in the words of Tammy Turtle, "If you want to learn how to write better poetry, study at the flippers of your favorite poets."

2. Keep your eyes and ears open. Ideas for poems are all around you. Write poetry about how an idea or your topic makes you feel.

3. Hunt for buried treasure in your early drafts of a poem. In other words, search for the often hidden, but special, idea in your rough draft. Then, make that idea grow by pouring details on it that readers can see.

4. Try using a figure of speech, such as a simile, in your poem. A simile compares unlike things using the word *like* or *as*.

5. Reread your poem many times both silently and aloud. Revise and edit your poem so that readers will understand what you're trying to say.

6. Celebrate poetry! It is meant to be read aloud, talked about, and shared. Think about framing your poem, as though it were a photograph or picture. Sammy Octopus likes to dress up his poems in wrapping paper and bows, and then give them to the special creatures in his life.

Key Points!

If you want to write better poetry, read and listen to a sea of poetry. Before writing a poem, close your eyes and try to picture your topic or idea; think about how your idea makes you feel. Then, write your poem so that readers will see the same picture in their minds that you see in yours and feel the same way you do about your topic.

Wrapping It Up!

Revising and celebrating are not the last steps in writing. Awesome authors like you know that revising happens at every step. They also know that celebrating can happen early on; writers are free to share even their rough drafts with readers.

Writing is painless. If you decide to write a rough draft of your ideas, you are free to focus on your message (what you are trying to say). Later, during revising, you can decide on the best way to get your message across. Then, if you're still not happy with what you've written, you can go back and forth between drafting and revising until your writing says just what you want it to say. Writing is painless.

As we've seen in this chapter, a beginning draft of a poem might not sound like anything special. Often, however, poets can find something special in a first draft. They then can build on that special idea by adding details to it that readers can see and feel.

Let's Try It!

Set #5

Write a poem about a topic of your choice, such as your favorite color, a mosquito that keeps biting you, someone in your life, a special place, a memory you have . . . anything you want. Your poem does not have to rhyme, but it can if you want it to.

Chapter 4

A Whale of a Tale: Story Writing

Everyone loves a good story. Here's one about an unusual rabbit named Jay Jay.

Jay Jay, the Roller-Skating Rabbit

Wahoo! Y-e-s! I've won the Carrot Cup! This sports trophy means more to me than the whole vegetable garden.

You see . . . I'm a rabbit who has never been able to hop. The Carrot Cup reminds me that I've trained hard and done my best. At last, I'm Jay Jay, the Roller-Skating Rabbit!

Growing up I often felt discouraged and disappointed. "Why can't I hop around the parsley patch like other bunnies?" I'd wonder. "It's not fair!"

Mom always tried to cheer me up and make me feel good about myself. "Everything will be fine, my little dandelion," she'd say. "You have beautiful, long teeth for chewing and excellent eyesight from eating all those carrots. You can even play the piano as well as Beethoven."

Yet, in spite of Mom's efforts, I remained down in the dumps.

Then, one sunny day, a woman wearing a purple blouse and pink and white polka dot knee-length shorts knocked on our door. Peeking out from behind Mom's apron I couldn't help but smile, as I noticed the roller-skating charms that dangled from her bracelet. The charms clanged together like wind chimes every time she moved her wrist.

"Hello, my name is Miss Wheels," said the friendly woman. "I hear you're looking for a babysitter." Just then, Miss Wheels spotted me. (I was crouched down, hiding behind my mom.) "Oh! And you must be Jay Jay!" she exclaimed. "What beautiful grayish-brown fur you have." (My fur also has specks of white in it, which Miss Wheels couldn't see from where she was standing.)

Mom and Miss Wheels sat at the kitchen table and talked about me for a long time—so long that I ate a basketful of celery while waiting for them to finish. After their chat, Mom hired Miss Wheels to be my babysitter.

Miss Wheels did everything a babysitter could do to make a bunny feel loved. She brushed my fur every day and read me stories about amazing animals. She took me to the Forest Fair, where we played games and sipped carrot shakes through straws. She even made my favorite dessert: spinach pudding. "De-lish!"

Nothing seemed to help, until one day when Miss Wheels took me to a sporting goods store and bought me special sneakers that were fitted with four, small wheels. (It just so happens that Miss Wheels is a roller-skating coach, as well as a babysitter.) Ever since that day, I've had a deep longing to roller skate.

I can still remember my first time on skates. It took me months to control my balance, not to mention all the flops I took. Once, I even got caught in the middle of a multiskater pile-up (that's when your legs become so tangled with other skaters that you can't tell which legs are yours). Thank goodness for fur! It helped cushion my falls. Thank goodness for helmets, elbow and knee pads, and wrist guards. They protected me from bruises and scratches.

Now, I roller skate anywhere and everywhere that's safe. As Miss Wheels always says, "Safety comes first!"

Today, as I relax on my sofa, I see my reflection in the shiny, silver-plated Carrot Cup. It reminds me that I'm not the best or the fastest skater in the rink, but I am a skater who always does his best. It reminds me that I'm not the hoppiest bunny in the parsley patch but, at last, I am definitely one of the happiest!

NAMING YOUR SHIP: TITLE

Although it is usually made up of only a few words, a title can be as powerful as a big wave. It invites readers into the story and makes them wonder what's ahead.

Think about yourself as a writer. Do you come up with a title before writing your story? Or, do you write your story and then think of a name for it? The painless news is that it doesn't matter which you do first. You can title your story at any time.

Writers like you often come up with many titles for their stories and then pick and choose the ones that work best. Take, for example, the story at the beginning of this chapter: "Jay Jay, the Roller-Skating Rabbit." Other possible titles for this piece are "A Rabbit Learns to Roller Skate" and "Hop-less, Not Hopeless." However, "Why Rabbit Can't Hop" would not be a good title choice because no reasons are given in the story as to why the animal is unable to hop.

Let's Try It!

Set #6

Directions: Below you will find five titles. Some of them fit the story about Jay Jay (the rabbit who cannot hop), and others do not. Write "Yes" in the space given if you think the title matches the rabbit story. Write "No" if you think it does not. The first one has been done for you.

1. Eating Celery   No
    If you as a reader came across the title "Eating Celery," would you find it exciting or catchy? Probably not, right? Also, although Jay Jay does eat celery while waiting for Miss Wheels and his mom to finish talking, his doing so is only a small event in the story.

2. It's a Bird . . . It's a Plane . . . It's a Roller-Skating Rabbit!   _____

3. Carrot Shakes   _____

4. Miss Wheels Teaches a Special Rabbit How to Roller Skate   _____

5. Skating Through Sadness into Gladness   _____

Directions: Complete the next activity by doing what is asked of you.

6. Read any three stories and invent a new title for each one. Make sure that your made-up title fits the story.

SEA CONDITIONS: SETTING

Setting is more than the time and place in which a story happens. It sets the mood for the whole writing piece.

Let's pretend that you're itching to write a great story. (Well, you're not really itching.) You want most of the action in your story to take place one hundred years ago in a dark, dusty house. The mood of your piece, then, will most likely be gloomy (sad) or scary. One of your characters might have hair that looks like cobwebs.

Now, try changing the setting, but leave everything else about your story the same. This time, make your story happen in current times (now), at an amusement park on a sunny day. The mood of your piece will most likely be lively and cheerful. Here, one of your characters might cling or stick to other people like cotton candy.

By changing just the setting, you can change the way your readers see the events that are happening in your writing piece and thereby change how they feel about them.

Usually, writers show details about the setting early in the story. They choose a setting based on wherever they want the action to occur. Here are a few examples of where a story might take place: desert, countryside, farm, town, city, village, school, home, ocean, forest, mountains, or outer space. The story could happen in the past, present, or future.

Key Points!
A setting is as important to a story as water is to a swimming pool. Think about and plan the details of your setting.

MARINE CREATURES: CHARACTERS

A story without characters is like a hot fudge sundae without ice cream. It is missing the main part.

Characters are the people or animals in a story. Readers do not meet them face to face, but they learn about them through the writer's descriptions. Good writers know how to make their characters come alive.

When writing about the characters in your story, describe both what they look like on the outside and what they think or feel on the inside. Try to give readers details about your characters, such as

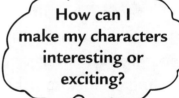

How can I make my characters interesting or exciting?

✔ **what they look like or wear**

✔ **how they talk and what they say**

✔ **how they act**

✔ **what they think and feel**

✔ **what other characters say about them**

For example, instead of writing "Diane is funny" to describe one of your characters, you might write "What Diane loves most about herself is that she can make most anyone laugh—anytime."

Think about some of your favorite characters. What is it about them that you like or find interesting? By looking at how other writers build or shape their characters, you can get ideas for building ones of your own.

You can get ideas for characters anywhere. They can come from

- **out of the air, hitting you like a sudden gust of wind**

- **your imagination**

- **everyday people in your life.**

Your characters do not have to be superheroes for your story to be super. By carrying a notebook and pencil with you at all times, you can write down ideas for characters whenever you meet someone interesting.

Let's say that you come across an unusual woman in a toy store. She is a grown-up on the outside, but more like a kid on the inside. You smile to yourself, as you watch her play with every item in the store. Suddenly, this wanna-be kid trapped in a grown-up's body leaves the store, never again to be seen by you. How, then, can you base one of your story's characters on this all-too-quick meeting? You might think about making her a small or not-so-important character in your story, or you might take what you found interesting about her and add it to what you found special about someone else, thereby building a totally new character of your own.

Key Points!

Ideas for building characters of your own are all around you. They come from your imagination and from people you either know or meet in passing.

Be sure to describe both what your characters look like on the outside and what they think or feel on the inside.

Let's Try It!

Set #7

Reread "Jay Jay, the Roller-Skating Rabbit" on page 53. Using specific details from the story, describe Jay Jay and Miss Wheels. In your writing, be sure to include details such as what the characters look like or wear; how they act, think, and feel; and what they say.

TROUBLE AT SEA: PROBLEM

Imagine this. You have the perfect setting in mind for a story: snow-covered mountains that invite children's playfulness and giggles. You also have amazing characters that excite readers. But there's one problem: You don't have a problem in mind for your story, and, without a problem, there is no story.

Readers long for action—for things to happen—on the page. Cheerful snow-covered mountains and interesting characters alone cannot hold their attention. Writers must think of ways to invite conflict (problem) into their pieces.

The mountains, for example, could cause a problem for one of the characters (maybe someone will get stuck while climbing them). Or the characters could have problems with each other, or even with themselves (maybe someone will tease or bully another person in the story, or characters will struggle with decisions that they, themselves, have to make, like whether they should climb the mountain).

Coming up with conflicts for your stories can be fun. You can play with different conflicts until you find the one that not only gets your story moving, but keeps it moving.

Writers get ideas for conflicts by using their imaginations and also by observing the world around them. Take your school, for example. I'll bet disagreements pop up in your classroom about everyday happenings, such as students cutting in line. Adults have disagreements, too. The point is that writers have their imaginations and a whole world from which to draw to get ideas for story conflicts.

Let's Try It!

Set #8

What is the conflict or problem in "Jay Jay, the Roller-Skating Rabbit" (pages 53–55)?

HELP HAS ARRIVED: SOLUTION

The conflict, or problem, in a story must somehow get solved. Readers stay with a good story until the end so they can see how the problem gets solved.

Often writers know ahead of time how they will solve their stories' conflicts. By planning a solution before writing your story, you will have a road map that can keep you from getting lost when you are writing. Yet, as we have learned throughout this book, there is no one right way to write that will work for every one of us all the time.

Sometimes, as we write, our stories take on lives of their own. During those times, we may decide to ignore our earlier plans and just go with the flow—that is, go wherever our writing takes us. Then, we may come up with a solution at the last moment—that is, as we're writing it.

In "Jay Jay, the Roller-Skating Rabbit," the conflict is solved when Jay Jay learns to roller skate. Can you come up with other ideas for solving the same conflict? Here are a few:

✔ **Jay Jay might find a rabbit doctor who could cure his problem.**

✔ **Jay Jay might spend the rest of his life at a camp for special wildlife, where he will learn to accept himself as he is. (Miss Wheels could be the camp counselor or the wildlife rehabilitator.)**

✔ **Jay Jay might find a friend in the forest who is willing to carry him around, as though he were a child.**

It's up to you as the writer to decide how best to solve the conflict in your story. Readers do not have to agree with your solution. They just have to feel as though their important questions have been answered.

BENEATH THE WAVES WITH WHO? POINT OF VIEW

In "Jay Jay, the Roller-Skating Rabbit," readers learn about what happens in the story through Jay Jay's eyes. This story is told from his point of view—from the way he sees the events that are taking place. Yet, it also could have been written from someone else's point of view—such as a narrator's or Miss Wheel's.

As a writer, you can choose from whose point of view you want your story to be told. By changing the point of view, you can change how readers see the characters or events in a story. If, for example, a narrator were telling the story about Jay Jay, and that narrator thought Jay Jay was spoiled, readers might feel differently about this amazing rabbit.

Wrapping It Up!

There is no one right way to write a story. Yet, stories do have elements in common, such as

- setting
- character(s)
- conflict (problem)
- events or happenings
- a solution

If you, as a writer, take the time to make these elements exciting, readers will take the time to turn your pages. They will become involved in your story and enjoy making guesses about what is going to happen next. They will see you as the awesome author you are!

Let's Try It!

Set #9

1. Using what you've learned so far about story elements— such as title, setting, characters, conflict, solution, and point of view—write a story of your own. If you need help, reread the information about story elements in this chapter.

2. Challenge: Here's a true story that you may have read about or seen on TV. A married couple found and rescued a squirrel that had been thrown out of its nest during a hurricane. They adopted the squirrel, named her Twiggy, and taught her how to water-ski and show off her talents in front of large audiences.

Some people think that it is mean to keep a wild animal like a squirrel as a pet even if it is injured (hurt). Others think that it is mean to send an injured animal back into the wild, where it may not be able to care for or protect itself.

What do YOU think? Please write at least two paragraphs about whether or not animals like Twiggy, the water-skiing squirrel, should be set free. Use the following chart to help you organize your thoughts before writing. Share your writing with others, and try to understand how they feel about the topic.

Reasons for Setting a Wild Animal Free	Reasons for Keeping a Wild Animal as a Pet
	The animal doesn't have to worry about food and shelter.

Chapter 5

Exploring Beginnings and Endings

CATCHY BEGINNINGS

Sammy Octopus is writing a story about a zebra. Here's how his piece begins.

One regular Friday a zebra, who hated the food served at her zoo, escaped. She ended up charging into the lunchroom of a nearby elementary school, in a mad search for pizza, while the kids were eating.

Did the beginning of Sammy's story grab your attention?

The lead, or the beginning of a piece of writing, has to catch the reader's eye right away. Yet, not every lead has to be as shocking as a zebra in a school lunchroom. Depending on the piece you are writing, any lead that is well written and that builds on itself can also get you off to a great start. Let's look at an example of a less shocking beginning.

Does your school have a day when many classes get together and take part in activities like tug-of-war, soccer, jolly ball, and the kangaroo hop? Our school does, and it's called Field Day.

Usually I have the best time at Field Day, and I go home with so many medals and ribbons that my bedroom transforms into a Sports Hall of Fame. But this year, something happened that ruined my whole day. This something could happen to anyone, but if you know about it ahead of time, you can save yourself a whole lot of trouble.

The beginning of the story about Field Day is not loud like thunder, but the topic—and the way that it is described—is attention grabbing. Each sentence in the lead builds on the one before and draws readers closer into the story, until the conflict (problem) hits them smack in the face and they cannot turn back. Readers want to find out what happened to the writer on Field Day, and how they can stop that same thing from ruining their own Field Day fun.

Read the next three different beginnings. Which one excites you the most and makes you want to read on?

- Last summer I went to visit Grandma. She lives in Arizona. We did a lot of fun things.
- I had a lot of fun last summer. I went to visit my sweet grandmother in Arizona. She cooked my favorite foods and bought me presents almost every day. It was fun being spoiled.
- Nine months have passed since I visited Grandma Grace in Arizona last summer. Yet, I can still taste her homemade brownies and apple pies. I can still see the balloon artist at the circus twisting a hat and dolphin for me.

I'll bet you liked the third lead the most. Most readers do. Let's zoom in on that beginning and talk about what makes it more interesting than the others.

The first two beginnings tell the events that happened last summer. Sentences like "We did a lot of fun things" and "I had a lot of fun last summer" are not exciting and do not let readers in on the fun the writer had. The third beginning shows the events of last summer through the use of specific details, such as an artist twisting balloons into a hat and a dolphin. Readers feel as though they are right there, alongside the writer, visiting grandma; it's more fun for them that way, so they read on.

Key Points!

Pssst. Here's a secret. Sammy Octopus and other authors write their beginnings last. That secret may sound strange, but it's true. Sammy waits until he has most of his story finished before working on his beginning.

In this way, he makes sure that his opening lines fit or lead nicely into the rest of his story.

It's up to you to decide the best time to write your leads. If you happen to come up with a great beginning before you write the rest of your piece, that's fine. Sammy Octopus promised that this book was going to be painless, and Sammy always keeps his promises.

Get Off to a Great Start

You can learn to write great beginnings from other authors, including your classmates. Read aloud the beginnings from your favorite books, and notice how they are written. When you come across leads that thrill you like a ride in a hot air balloon, write them in your notebook. Ask yourself, "Why did the author begin this way? What is it about this lead that makes me want to read on?" Then, take what you learned from the author, and use it to write great starts of your own.

There are many ways to write beginnings. Here are some.

 Begin with action

Hopps began climbing the tall, wet ladder that led to his enchanted tree house. He had almost made it to the top rung when, suddenly, the ladder broke.

This lead gets readers wondering and thinking, "What happened to Hopps?" They read on to find out. Notice that the writer has started off in the middle of the action and has focused first on hooking readers. The details of what happened can be explained later, once the writer knows that readers are hooked.

✔ Open with dialogue or conversation

"It's tonsil-take-out time," said Dr. Paine, wearing a mask over his mouth.

"I'm outta here," screamed six-year-old Joshua, jumping out of bed and tearing up the hospital hallway in a mad dash for the elevators. "No way! Oh no! Not me! I don't care how big or infected they are. I'm not having my tonsils out! Ain't happenin'. I don't care if, after the surgery, I can eat a truckload of ice cream."

By having the characters say interesting things, the writer of this lead lets readers see the important details. We feel almost as though we're running with Joshua down that hospital hallway. We continue reading to see what happens next, as we hope for the best for this frightened boy. (Here's a secret: The author of *Painless Junior Writing* had her tonsils taken out a few years ago, and it was as easy as riding a bike.)

✔ Start off with a sound effect

Creeeeak! As she was jumping up to score the winning basket in a tie game, Becky's knee gave out.

Doesn't this lead make you hear, or at least picture, the sound of Becky's knee cracking? It gives clues, or just enough details, to make readers feel extra sorry for Becky—given the bad timing of her knee problem. (Her knee gave out just as she was about to shoot the winning basket.)

Whether or not we play sports, we've all been in situations like Becky's. We're just about to save the day or we're so close to winning. But then, at the last moment, something happens, and the situation doesn't turn out as we'd planned. Becky is a character all of us can relate to or understand. We read on to see what happens and how she handles herself.

Pssst . . . Try to keep a list of noisy words that you come across in your reading. They will come in handy when you want to create sound effects in your writing. Here are a few *creeeaky* words to help you get started.

Crunch! There's nothing like crispy cereal to wake up everyone in the house, even Gizmo—our sleepyhead cat.

Dad jumps out of bed. His feet hit the floor. "*Smack!*" "*Bam!*" He runs to the kitchen.

"*Shhh!*" he says to me. Please crunch quietly. I don't want to wake up the neighbors and their pets, too. The last thing I need is for them to *bang* their fists on our newly painted door.

Gizmo comes over to me. "Argh!" he grunts. Next time, I'll know better than to get in the way of a cat's beauty sleep.

Begin with a surprising question

Have you ever fallen or jumped into a swimming pool with your clothes on? And then, Uh-oh, your parents give you a look that screams, "You're in big trouble."

Readers, young and old, can relate to and enjoy this lead. Many of us have somehow ended up in a pool, wearing our clothes. Young readers know the "you're-in-big-trouble" look, and the wording of it as "a look that screams" is catchy.

 ## Begin with a surprising sentence

If you swallow a wad of bubble gum, it will stay in your stomach for about six years.

Does this sentence make you wonder? Is the writer telling you the truth or just joking with you? You'll have to read on to find out.

 ## Introduce an interesting character

Trevor was a regular kid. He loved sports, especially baseball; rode his bike wherever he could; and liked to hang out with his friends. Only one thing about Trevor was different—so different that it won him a place in the Guinness Book of World Records.

Are you thinking what I'm thinking? What is so different about Trevor that makes him a record holder? Does he have the longest tongue, or does he hold the record for the fastest speed on a snowmobile or skateboard? We don't know, but we want to know; so we read on to find out. Notice, too, that this lead—like others you might come across in your reading—tricks us as readers, to get our attention. It starts out by naming all the things that make Trevor a "regular" kid—and then, Boom! We learn that he holds a world record.

If all this talk and fuss about writing good beginnings is beginning to sound painful, don't worry: It is not.

Yes! Beginnings are one of the most important parts of your writing. You will have to practice writing and revising them. But with time and practice, you will be able to write opening sentences that glue readers to your pages.

Key Points!

Every beginning does not have to be award winning or show stopping. Your opening should give readers just enough details to keep them guessing or wondering, so they'll read on and be hooked on your every word.

Let's Try It!

Set #10

This chapter gave you painless ways to write catchy beginnings or leads:

- Begin with action.
- Open with dialogue or conversation.
- Start off with a sound effect.
- Begin with a surprising question.

- Begin with a surprising sentence.
- Introduce an interesting character.

For each way given, come up with your own catchy beginning. Reread the examples in the chapter if you need help.

STAR ENDINGS

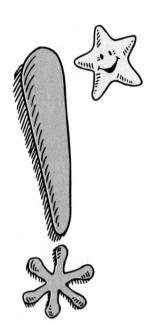

Have you ever watched a movie that had a great beginning and middle, but whose ending let you down? No matter how much you liked the movie up until those final moments or scenes, you remember the boring ending more than anything else.

Key Points!

Endings matter! Because they are the last thing that readers see, they are as important as beginnings. But this is no reason to worry about writing them. Here's the painless news: Your ending does not have to wow the socks off the reader; it just has to be right for the piece you are writing.

It doesn't matter if your ending is cheerful, sad, shocking, or anything in between—as long as it satisfies readers. An ending, or conclusion, wraps up the loose ends in the writing piece and answers many of the important questions readers may have. A good ending to a good story makes readers feel as though they've just eaten a good meal. And that's a good feeling.

Writers think about endings long before they write them. It sounds strange, but writers think about endings from the beginning—that is, from early on in their writing. By not waiting until the last moment to figure out how they will conclude their pieces, writers avoid getting stuck.

Let's look at two different endings for an essay on Thomas Jefferson.

1. As I said before, Jefferson was a great man and president. He did wonderful things for our country. For example, he was a signer of the Declaration of Independence. We owe a lot to him.

2. Not only was Thomas Jefferson the third president of the United States, but he was also a founding father of our country and a man of the people. Americans enjoy many freedoms today due to Jefferson's hard work and genius. Thank you, Mr. Jefferson, for serving America for fifty years.

Which of the endings do you think is better? Ending # 2, right? Now, let's mix things up a little. Instead of talking about why Ending #2 is better, we'll focus on Ending #1 and try to figure out what it is about that ending that makes it not as good as the second one.

Notice the opening words in Ending #1: "As I said before." Readers can become bored when you tell them you're going to repeat something that you've already said. Notice also the third sentence in Ending #1: "For example, he was a signer of the Declaration of Independence." Such an example belongs in the main part of the essay, rather than in the conclusion (ending).

A GREAT FINISH

When it comes to writing endings, it helps to know what NOT to do.

- Do not use phrases like: *in conclusion, to conclude, in summary, as I said before,* or *as I already mentioned.*
- Do not repeat information that you used in the beginning unless you are doing so to create a special effect for readers.
- Do not tell readers things they already know, such as airplanes fly or babies cry.

There are many types, or kinds, of endings. The list below shows you a few and gives you painless tips on how to write each of them, as well as examples.

Surprise Ending: A surprise ending catches the reader off guard, but it also makes sense.

> **Painless Tip:** If you want the ending of your piece to surprise readers, begin planning it early in your writing. Try to give readers hints along the way about the surprise to come.

> **Example**
> Sammy Octopus has moved. His new address is 1600 Pennsylvania Avenue, Washington, D.C. He lives in a H-U-G-E aquarium in the Blue Room.
>
> Although he misses his old cave and his friends, Sammy has a lot of new friends and students. He is teaching writing to pets belonging to the president and other workers at the White House.
>
> Sammy plans to return to sea one day—that is, if he doesn't decide to run for president.

Funny Ending: Another type of ending makes the reader giggle.

> **Painless Tip:** Hunt for the funniest part(s) in your piece. Try to tie that part into your ending, but use different words or details.

> **Example**
>
> Sammy is still sleepless at sea. Schools of misbehaving fish continue to play loud games of tag outside his cave. These on-the-go vertebrates are causing him to become as grouchy as a sourpuss. Imagine that, an octopus that is a sourpuss—and, a red one at that (he's red because he's mad). As much as he doesn't want to move, Sammy is going to find a quieter resting spot in the ocean.

Return-to-the-Beginning Ending: Like a circle, this ending ends at the same point or place it started.

> **Painless Tip:** Often, this type of ending is planned early on in your writing.

> **Example**
>
> Sammy's daughter, Elinore, is a grown octopus who loves to write. As a kid, she didn't like writing.
>
> While growing up in the Pacific Ocean, Elinore spent too much time on her waterproof cell phone, sending photographs back and forth to her friends. When she wasn't on the phone, she was at the Tide Runner Mall, shopping and spending her allowance. Luckily, she has eight arms to carry home all the clothes and shoes that she bought.
>
> Then, one cheerful day at sea, Elinore's real-life fairy godmother—Mindy Mind—bought her a book called *Painless Junior Writing*. A chapter later, Elinore hopped on board the fun ship *Authorship*, and her life has never been the same.

Wrapping It Up!

If you as a writer want readers to stick with you through the pages, take the time to write beginnings and endings that stick with them through the ages. Writing is painless. You can begin a piece of writing in many ways, such as with

✔ **action**
✔ **a sound effect**
✔ **a surprising question or sentence**
✔ **an interesting character**

Sometimes it is easier to write your opening lines last, once you've seen how your piece has turned out.

Writing is painless. You can end a piece of writing in many ways, such as by surprising readers or making them laugh. Like a great beginning, a great ending does not have to be larger than life; it just has to be the right one for the piece you're writing.

Let's Try It!

Set #11

Reread the endings of some of your favorite books, stories, or other pieces, including those written by your classmates. Try to find examples of the kinds of endings listed above: surprise, funny, and return-to-the-beginning.

As you are reading, try to figure out what the writer is doing to make the ending stick in the reader's mind. Then, think about how you might use what you learned to improve one of your own endings.

Chapter 6

Playing with Words

WORD MAGIC (A FAIRY TALE)

A while back, in the library of an underwater castle, a book that was dressed in rainbow colors felt as sad as someone whose best friend had just moved away.

"Why don't young fish read me or check me out of the castle library?" asked the colorful book to its caring librarian, Mrs. Whisper.

Mrs. Whisper answered in her usual soft-spoken voice, "Your colors are friendly, but your author—Mr. Ruff Draft—didn't care about his word choices. So, your pages have the most unexciting words I have ever seen in my 333 years of being a librarian. They make young fish and even older fish want to snooze."

"You are right," said the lonely book. "I have seen young fish asleep on the coral reef reading carpet. Can you think of a way to make my words more exciting?"

"I will certainly try," whispered Mrs. Whisper. "Maybe the king of our underwater castle—King Sammy, the Writing Octopus—can lend a helping tentacle. He rules the A-B-Seas of Writing."

Mrs. Whisper darted off and found King Sammy. She told him that readers in the library castle were snoring because words in a book were boring.

"Not to worry," replied the kind king. Then he added this rhyming sentence: "We'll make the words alluring, rather than boring, and readers will no longer be snoring!"

The next day, King Sammy met up with the book's author, Mr. Ruff Draft. He asked him to think about changing the dull words that were causing all the sea monster snores in the library. To everyone's surprise, Mr. Ruff Draft refused. "No!" he roared like the ocean on a stormy night. He didn't like young fish, and he wasn't about to do anything to help those noisy, little, slimy creatures (as he called them).

The king was horrified by such name calling. He loved all the young fish that darted about in the misty blue-green waters of the castle. Unlike Mr. Ruff Draft, the king would do anything to help young fish. (The wise king knew that young fish are our future.)

King Sammy knew exactly what to do. He sprinkled seven pounds of word-magic dust onto Mr. Ruff Draft. Within seconds, Mr. Ruff Draft was transformed into Mr. Wise-to-Revise. And, so he began the voyage to more exciting reading!

Together with the king, Mr. Wise-to-Revise tossed the lifeless words used by Mr. Ruff Draft into the landfill and called aboard ones that were alive, juicy, and alluring. A short time later, young fish were found staying up past their bedtimes to read the new book with its attention-grabbing words. There were no more sleepy young fish in the library.

And they all lived, and they all read and wrote, happily ever after—including Mr. Wise-to-Revise, who went on to write 777 exciting books.

Let's Try It!

Set #12

1. What did the fairy tale teach you about reading and writing? Use details from the fairy tale to support your answer.

2. Pretend you are King Sammy. Write a letter to the author, Mr. Ruff Draft, explaining why it is important for writers to make wise word choices. Sign your letter King Sammy, the Writing Octopus.

PICTURE GAMES: PAINTING A WORD PICTURE

Have you ever read a book that you didn't want to put down? I'll bet the writer of that book made you feel excited, interested, and involved—almost as if you were part of the story's action. Good writers use words to paint a picture inside the reader's head. They help readers "see" the events that are happening in the story.

As you write, you have ideas in your mind that you want to share with readers. Words are the only tools you have to get those ideas across. Like a puppy or kitten, the words you put on a page need care and attention. If you choose blah words, your writing will be blah. If, however, you use the right words in the right way, your writing will sizzle and pop. Choose your words carefully!

Below you will find a paragraph titled "The Big Horse." Then you will see three different pictures of horses.

1. Read the paragraph.

2. Look at the three different pictures of the horses and see if you can tell which picture the writer of the paragraph is trying to describe.

 Happy Hint: The writer does not make wise words choice, so you may not be able to see a clear picture in your mind.

The Big Horse

Today I saw a horse in a field. It was a big horse. It was near a fence. It was alone. Maybe one day I'll ride horses.

Which picture is the writer of "The Big Horse" trying to describe?

Horse #1   Horse #2   Horse #3

If you had trouble guessing which picture the writer was trying to describe, you are not alone. Now you see why it is important for writers to word things just the right way. Otherwise, the reader can become as confused as a mouse in a maze.

IT MAKES SENSE TO USE YOUR SENSES: DESCRIPTIVE WRITING

Key Points!
You can write more interesting and detailed descriptions if you use your five senses. Great authors, like you, remember sights, sounds, tastes, smells, and textures (how something feels) around them. They also use their senses when they write to create a movie in the reader's mind.

Let's look closely at the picture of the horse eating grass in the field.

Use the graphic organizer below to help you describe the horse in the picture.

Sights	Sounds	Tastes	Smells	Textures	Other Important Details
	Example: sound of the horse munching and chomping on the crisp grass			Example: feel of the horse's mane or tail	Example: what the picture makes you think of

Let's Try It!

Set #13

Using the information from your graphic organizer, write a descriptive paragraph about the horse in the picture. Be sure to use all five senses as you write. Reread your paragraph and make sure it describes the picture. Check your writing for errors in spelling, capitalization, and punctuation. Share your paragraph with friends and family members.

Now that you're on your way to becoming a wizard at painting word pictures, let's try again using horse blankets as our topic. Read the paragraph below titled "A Blanket for My Horse." Think about the picture the writer is trying to create in your head. READY . . . SET . . . TROT . . . GALLOP!

A Blanket for My Horse

I bought a beautiful blanket for my horse to wear. It makes me think of the sky because it has suns, moons, and stars on it. The suns are my favorite. When I put this long, pretty blanket on my horse, he and I will be proud.

Can you tell which of the following blankets the writer is trying to describe?

A

B

C

Again, when a writer does not make wise word choices, readers don't always see the picture the writer wants them to see. So, it is hard to tell which of the three blankets the writer is trying to describe.

Let's trot on! Read the next paragraph titled "A One-of-a-Kind Saddle Blanket." See if you can figure out which of the three blankets the writer is describing.

A One-of-a-Kind Saddle Blanket

When I showed my friend the saddle blanket that I bought for my horse, Galaxy, she couldn't stop saying, "Ooh! Aah!"

A crescent moon and two suns light up the middle section of the blanket. Four stars, one in each corner, glow on the fabric like Rudolph's nose. Two horizontal stripes separate the suns and moon from the stars.

Now, all I need to do is find a matching head stall, and my horse will get more attention than the ice cream truck on a sizzling day.

This time, I'm sure you were able to see a picture of the blanket in your mind because the writer used clear language. So, "A One-of-a-Kind Saddle Blanket" is about Blanket B.

Let's Try It!
Set #14

Choose one of the other two blankets (Blanket A or C), and write a descriptive paragraph about the part of the blanket that you see in the drawing. Remember to be a good observer and write in detail what you see. When you are done, have your classmates or family members read your description and see if they can figure out which blanket you are describing.

CATCH THE EXCITEMENT: LANDING ON JUST-RIGHT WORDS

Read the next story about a special horse named Dusty.

Dusty

Clickety-clack, clickety-clack . . . those are the sounds that greet me first thing every morning. Clickety-clack.

Still half asleep, I reach for my binoculars on the dresser and make my way into the living room, stopping for some chocolate milk along the way. By now I am fully awake. With binoculars in hand, I gaze through the window of my cottage, which overlooks a training school for horses. This has been my routine every day for the past ten years. Horse watching is my favorite hobby.

This morning, when I looked through my window, I saw a horse standing all by itself, near a post-and-rail rectangular fence that closes in the land belonging to the training school. "That's strange," I said to myself, wondering why the horse was alone.

My curiosity got the best of me. I got dressed quickly and left my cottage. When I reached the closed-in fence area, I approached the lone horse carefully, patted his neck, and said, "Why do you look sad?" He kept staring at the other horses that were learning how to walk, trot, canter, gallop, and obey signals.

So I said, "You want to be with them and learn all the lessons perfectly, don't you? You want to be in the horse show in New York?" He looked at me and gave a nudge.

Heading for the main office of the training school, I asked the first instructor I came across if he knew why my new friend looked sad. He said, "Oh, that's Dusty. He failed his entry test. He's staying with us until his owner can come get him. That should be in about a month."

Later that afternoon I walked over to Dusty and said, "I have a plan . . . a way to be part of the group. Each morning we will observe the other horses carefully as they do their routines. Then we'll practice and do our own workouts." Dusty clacked his teeth and nodded his head. He was ready for the challenge ahead of him.

After three weeks I begged the head instructor at the training school to give Dusty another chance, which he did. Dusty passed with flying colors. He shuffled his hooves as if to thank me.

I left the cottage for several weeks to go on a business trip. When I returned, I bought a local newspaper to catch up with the latest goings-on. To my surprise, on the front page of the newspaper was a photograph of Dusty. He had won the Apple-Red Ribbon!

From the way Dusty's nose was crinkled in the newspaper photo, I could tell he was saying "thank you" to me. From the way his mane flowed like a flag in the wind, I could tell he was mighty proud of himself.

The next time I saw Dusty, he looked at me and said, "Y-a-y! Studying and concentration leads to success." Then, he trotted off and headed straight for the bushel of apples in his stable.

(An Afterword: Dusty says, "Always wear a riding helmet!")

The writer of "Dusty" used dialogue to move the story along. Dialogue is the talking that takes place between the characters in a story. Did you notice a word that the writer used each time the characters were talking to each other? Reread the story again and see if you can find it.

If you said "said," you are correct. Let's look at a sentence from "Dusty."

> When I reached the closed-in fence area, I approached the lone horse carefully, patted his neck, and said, "Why do you look sad?"

Can you think of a more descriptive word for "said" here? How about replacing it with either **"whispered"** or **"asked"**?

> When I reached the closed-in fence area, I approached the lone horse carefully, patted his neck, and *whispered*, "Why do you look sad?"

> When I reached the closed-in fence area, I approached the lone horse carefully, patted his neck, and *asked*, "Why do you look sad?"

Whispered and *asked* are synonyms for said. A synonym is a word that has the same meaning, or almost the same meaning, as another word.

Careful!

Should we bury easy words like *said*, *good*, and *happy*? Sammy says, "No, because good writers are happy to use them in their writing at times."

If *said*, *good*, and *happy* are the best word choices for your paper, then the coast is clear for you to use them. Just be careful not to overuse them or overuse any word, unless you are trying to create a special effect for the reader.

In this chapter, we said goodbye to wrestling with words and hello to playing with them. We learned that it's okay to use everyday words like *said* and *good*, as long as they work well in our writing.

Before you put just any thoughts on your final paper, take some time and think. Look for words that say just what you want them to say and that will help readers understand your message.

Wrapping It Up!

Making wise word choices is painless. You have millions of words to play with, and you are free to use everyday words like *nice* and *said* if they're the best ones for the piece you're writing.

By choosing your words and sentences carefully, you will help readers see clear pictures in their heads. And, readers will see you as the word wiz you are.

Let's Try It!

Set #15

Get ready to have fun surfing!

Each of the surfboards below has a word written in it. For each word, write two synonyms in the space given. Use a dictionary or thesaurus if you need help. The first one has been done for you.

 Happy Hint: A synonym is a word that has the same, or almost the same, meaning as another word.

happy   cheerful _____   merry _____

sad _____   _____

big _____ _____

little _____ _____

nice _____ _____

great _____ _____

good _____ _____

bad _____ _____

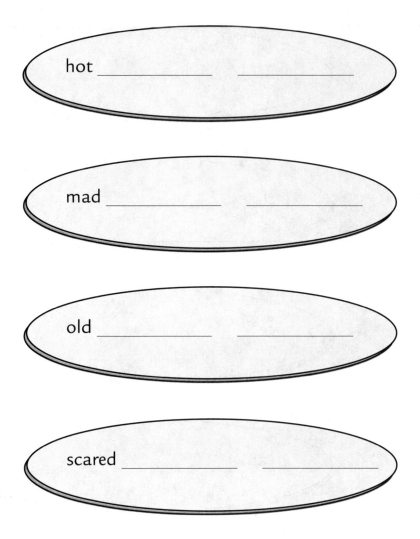

hot _____ _____

mad _____ _____

old _____ _____

scared _____ _____

Chapter 7

Scoring with Parts of Speech

HOME-RUN VERBS

One of the best ways to hit a home run with your pen or pencil is to use strong action words. See if you can spot some of them as you read the next story.

Smashing, Sliding, and Scoring

No one is luckier than I. Not only did my favorite baseball team, the Green Socks, win the playoffs, but my dad bought me tickets to see them clobber the Purple Jays in the opening game of the World Series.

And clobber they did!

One by one, the great Green Socks' batters hammered balls all over the playing field (and outside it, too). They slammed and smashed; they cracked and crushed. They bashed ball after ball. The scoreboard worked overtime whenever the Green Socks stepped like warriors up to the plate.

One can only imagine the wild locker-room dance that the Green Socks did that night to celebrate their win.

No one is luckier than the Green Socks' players.

I'm sure you spotted a lot of action or doing words in the story, such as *clobber*, *hammered*, *slammed*, *smashed*, *cracked*, *crushed*, and *bashed*. You may know that these words are called verbs. Now here's the hot fudge topping on your banana split: By using strong verbs in your writing, you can keep your readers as excited as baseball fans reaching for a foul ball.

Most verbs show action or describe what someone or something is doing; however, not all verbs are alike. Some are weak and do not create pictures in the readers' mind. Others are strong and give readers details they may need to know. *Walked* is a weak verb because it does not show readers how the action was done. *Raced* is a strong, home-run verb because it shows how someone or some-thing walked.

Example

Weak Verb: Sean *walked* home after the fifth inning.

Strong Verb: Sean *raced* home after the fifth inning.

By using the home-run verb *raced*, the writer paints a picture of Sean speeding home like a jet plane, rather than taking his time and strolling home.

Now, get ready to move about and "act out" some verbs. On your mark, get set, go! *Hop* on one foot. Now, *stomp* your feet. Good! Now, pretend you're an airplane and *fly* or *soar* above the clouds. Super! Now, get out of the way of a wild pitch. I mean *dodge, escape,* or *duck* a wild pitch. Fantastic! Take a deep breath and relax. You have felt the difference between action-packed verbs like *dodge* or *duck,* and lifeless ones like *get.*

You are well on your way to hitting a grand-slam home run with verbs. Look at the two sentences below. One uses a weak verb, and the other uses a strong one. Which sentence do you think creates a better picture in the reader's mind?

Sentence #1: The pitcher *was* sad.

Sentence #2: Tears *streamed* down the pitcher's face.

If you chose Sentence #2, *smile, skip,* and *jump* up and down ten times. By using the strong verb *streamed,* the writer guides readers to see and feel the pitcher's sadness. Now that's home-run writing!

Careful!
Whenever you can, and whenever it makes sense to do so, use strong verbs in your writing. However, there will be times when a weaker verb is either the best or the only word choice for your paper.

Let's Try It!

Set #16

Directions: Rewrite the sentences in 1 through 6 by changing the underlined weak verb into a strong one. Use a dictionary or thesaurus if you need help. The first one has been done for you. Note that there are many possible answers.

1. Weak Verb: The first baseman <u>hit</u> the ball over the fence in left field.

    Strong Verb: The first baseman <u>hammered</u> (<u>slammed</u>, <u>smashed</u>, or <u>cracked</u>) the ball over the fence in left field.

2. Weak Verb: Avery <u>is holding</u> the baseball.

    Strong Verb: _____

3. Weak Verb: Ned, Sam, and Joshua <u>left</u> the field.

    Strong Verb: _____

4. Weak Verb: Ariel and Caroline <u>were</u> happy when their team won.

    Strong Verb: _____

5. Weak Verb: Leaves <u>fell</u> onto the playing field.

    Strong Verb: _____

6. Weak Verb: Jonathan <u>ate</u> a hot dog and French fries at the baseball game.

    Strong Verb: _____

Directions: Complete the next question by doing what is asked of you.

7. Challenge: Find at least eight verbs in a newspaper or magazine, and circle them. Think about whether the verbs you've circled are strong or weak. If they're weak, try to replace them with strong, home-run verbs. Discuss your findings with a friend, and have a grand-slam home-run day!

TOUCHDOWN NOUNS

A noun is as important to a sentence as a helmet is to a football player. One way to score a touchdown with your pen or pencil is to use *specific* nouns, not general ones.

Examples

General Noun: <u>He</u> wants a <u>ball</u> for his birthday.

Specific Noun: <u>Marty</u> wants a <u>football</u> for his birthday.

General Noun: <u>They</u> want a <u>pet</u>.

Specific Noun: <u>Matt</u> and <u>Jennifer</u> want a blue-bearded <u>lizard</u>.

Specific nouns give readers details they may need to know. If it weren't for specific nouns, Marty might receive a baseball or basketball for his birthday (when he really wants a football), and Matt and Jennifer might receive a ferret (when they really want a lizard).

Now, you try. Look at the example below. Put a circle around the sentence that uses specific nouns.

Example

<u>Mattye</u> will feast on <u>cotton candy</u> and <u>ice cream</u>.

<u>She</u> will feast on <u>sweets</u>.

If you circled the sentence "Mattye will feast on cotton candy and ice cream," you are on your way to tackling nouns and scoring a touchdown.

Key Points!

Specific nouns can add lively details to your writing and help show readers what you are trying to say. Whenever it makes sense to do so, try to use specific, rather than general, nouns. By keeping specific nouns on the playing field and general nouns on the sideline, you will be on your way to scoring a touchdown with your writing.

Let's Try It!

Set #17

1. The paragraph below is about a football game, but because it uses so many general nouns, it sounds funny. Rewrite the paragraph by changing the bold general nouns into specific ones.

*Smack in the middle of an exciting football game, a **dog** began chasing the **player**. **They** could not believe their eyes. The animal tried to tug at the player's **hat** and **shoes**. Luckily, **people** came along carrying a huge bag of **food**. The food distracted the dog, and he left the player alone. **Everyone** roared.*

2. Challenge: Number a piece of paper from 1 to 10. Find ten nouns in your social studies textbook and write them on your paper. Label each noun as being either "general" or "specific." If you've labeled a noun as general, try to make it more specific.

THE MVPs: STRONG VERBS AND SPECIFIC NOUNS

Verbs and nouns are often the most important words a writer can use to get a message across to readers. If you want to score a home run or touchdown with your writing, try using strong verbs and specific nouns whenever you can. They are the **M**ost **V**aluable **P**layers (the **MVPs**).

What about adjectives—you know, those words that your teacher calls describing words? Do they belong on the court or on the bench? Let your eyes peer into the next section to find out.

ADJECTIVES AND POST-GAME HIGHLIGHTS

How do adjectives help writers paint a picture with words?

Happy Hint: Adjectives are italicized in the basketball phrases below.

red sneakers	*enormous* court
major penalty	*tall* player

Now you see why adjectives are often called describing words. They describe, or add more detail to, nouns and pronouns. Let's take a closer look at how they help writers paint word pictures.

Examples

The captain ordered uniforms for his team. (This sentence does not give readers a picture of what the uniforms looked like.)

The captain ordered *dark blue* and *white, striped* uniforms for his team. (The adjectives *dark blue*, *white*, and *striped* help readers see a clearer picture of the uniforms.)

Careful!

Using too many adjectives can litter your writing and make it sound funny. Choose your describing words carefully.

When faced with a weak sentence, try to improve the sentence first by adding stronger verbs and nouns. Then, if adjectives are still needed to make the writing more descriptive, carefully sprinkle a few onto the page.

The scoreboard below shows you how strong verbs, specific nouns, and carefully chosen adjectives can help you make it to the playoff games.

Type of Shot (Point(s) Earned)	Sentence
Free Throw (1 point)	She got the ball.
Lay-Up (2 points)	She got the round, leather ball.
Slam-Dunk (2 points with strong effect on fans and readers)	She grabbed the round, leather ball.
Three Pointer (3 points)	Darla grabbed the basketball.

Wrapping It Up!

Pow! Bam! Boom! Smack in the middle of a sentence, a verb jumped off the page and grabbed my attention. Verbs are the most powerful words that writers can use to get their messages across to readers. Adjectives, or describing words, are sometimes helpful, but be careful not to overuse them. Often, one strong verb or one specific noun is stronger than many adjectives strung together.

Now you have the ball and a chance to show off your skills by answering some bouncing Let's Try It! questions (on the following page).

Let's Try It!

Set #18

Directions: Use the scoreboard/chart on page 112 to answer questions 1 through 5. Write your answers using complete sentences. The first one has been done for you.

1. What is the weak verb that was used?

   Answer: The weak verb that was used is *got*, as in "She got the ball."

2. Why is *got* a weak verb? Explain what makes it weak?

3. *Round* and *leather* are adjectives that were used to describe the general noun, *ball*. Write three other describing words for *ball*.

4. What is the strong verb that was used? Explain what makes it powerful or what makes it the MVP—the Most Valuable Player?

5. What are the two specific nouns that were used?

Chapter 8

Play Like the Pros

SCORING WITH FIGURATIVE LANGUAGE

SIMILE

Writers sometimes use a figure of speech called a simile to grab a reader's attention. The magical chart below turns sentences that do not contain similes into ones that do. As you read the sentences, see if you can figure out what a simile is.

Not a Simile	Simile
Sarah's fingernail is long.	Sarah's fingernail is as long as a football field.
Readers remember good writing.	Good writing sticks to the reader's mind like peanut butter.
The strawberry was as red as an apple.	The strawberry was as red as a fire truck.
Terrence marched in the parade.	Terrence marched in the parade like a wind-up toy soldier.

Now that you've read the examples in the magic chart, can you explain in your own words what a simile is or does?

> ## Key Points!
> A **simile** compares unlike things in order to describe something, and it uses the words *like* or *as*.

Careful!

Not every sentence that has the word *like* or *as* in it contains a simile.

- "Marilyn and Tom like cats" is not a simile because it does not compare things in order to describe them. The word *like* in that sentence is a verb.
- "The strawberry was as red as an apple" is not a simile because the things being compared (strawberry and apple) are more alike than different. (They are both fruits.) A simile compares unlike things, such as a strawberry and a fire truck.

Similes are like the special effects in a movie; they help the audience see what is happening in a story, poem, or other writing piece. Try using similes to wake up your writing, but do not overuse them. Otherwise, they will lose their power and special effect.

Let's Try It!

Set #19

Directions: Use similes to complete sentences 1 through 5.

1. Sarah's fingernail is as short as _____ .

2. Mr. Nelson is as funny as _____ .

3. Writing is like _____ .

4. Felicia is as sweet as _____ .

5. Writing a paper without revising it is like _____ .

Happy Hint: Think of something that is hard or impossible to do.

Directions: Complete 6 through 8 by doing what is asked of you.

6. Similes are often found in songs and poems. Try to find at least four similes and write them down. Think about starting a simile collection.

7. Cut out four pictures from magazines or newspapers. Create a simile for each picture. Make sure you have permission to cut out the pictures before you do so; otherwise, the owner of the magazine or newspaper might be as angry as thunder (a simile).

8. Challenge: Is the sentence "Revising is Sammy's close friend" a simile? Why or why not? Use the definition (meaning) of a simile (on page 118) to help you explain your answer.

HYPERBOLE

If you want your writing to jump off the page and grab at your readers like an octopus, try using a figure of speech called a hyperbole (hi-PER-buh-lee). The magical chart below turns sentences that do not contain hyperboles into ones that do.

Not a Hyperbole	Hyperbole
Anthony blew a very large bubble.	Anthony blew such a large bubble that an elephant could fit inside it.
Ashley's eyelashes are very long.	Ashley's eyelashes are so long that she can put them in a ponytail.
The ferris wheel at the amusement park is big.	The ferris wheel at the amusement park is so big that it takes longer for it to go around once than it does for the earth to revolve around the sun (365 days).
The tennis player was sweating.	The tennis player was sweating so much that the fans thought it was raining.

Now that you've read the examples in the magic chart, can you explain in your own words what a hyperbole is or does?

A **hyperbole** is a figure of speech that stretches the truth. It is a wild exaggeration that is used to make your writing more descriptive.

Key Points!

Try to come up with new and fresh hyperboles, ones that readers have not seen before. Do not overuse hyperboles in your writing; otherwise, they will become tired and so will your readers.

Let's Try It!

Set #20

Directions: Complete sentences 1 through 6 by using hyperboles (exaggerations). Remember to s-t-r-e-t-c-h the truth!

Examples

- The bear ate barely enough food; he lost so much weight that now he can hula-hoop inside a doughnut.
- One million times a day, the lunchroom monitor orders the children in the cafeteria to keep their voices down.

1. It was so hot out today that _____.

2. Michelle has so many books in her house that _____.

3. Omar is such an awesome basketball player that _____.

4. It is so cold outside that _____.

5. Tara's eyelashes are so long that _____.

6. Her teeth sparkle so much that _____.

Directions: Complete 7 and 8 by doing what is asked of you.

7. Illustrate (draw) two or more of your favorite hyperboles.

8. Hyperboles are common in tall tales. Read some tall tales, and keep a list of all the hyperboles you find. I hope you have as much fun reading as a kitten playing in a room with a thousand balls of string on the floor.

SCORING WITH DETAILS THAT READERS CAN SEE

Add details to your writing . . . details, details, details. If you hear those words one more time, you might never add another detail to anything—not even another candle to your cake on your next birthday.

Don't worry. In this painless section, we won't talk about details in the same old way. We'll chat about them in a way that will make them come alive for you and for your readers. Take a peek at the next example.

Example

Sentence #1: The woman was old and she had a hard time walking.

Sentence #2: Holding onto a cane, the gray-haired woman—all wrapped up in wrinkles—placed one foot carefully in front of the other.

Which sentence helps you as a reader *see* what is happening? The second one, right? Notice how the two sentences differ. The first one tells you what to think or feel about the woman. The second one describes the woman and let's you figure out for yourself what the description means. It's more interesting that way.

Here's another example.

Example

Sentence #1: Ryan's backpack looks like a kangaroo's pouch.

Sentence #2: Ryan's backpack is big.

I'm sure you can tell which of the two sentences shows readers the details—the first one, right? Sentence #2 does not give readers a picture in their minds of the size of the backpack.

Like you, readers are smart and curious. They can become bored, and even annoyed, when a writer tells them what's happening in a piece. If you want to get and keep your readers' attention, let them *see* the important details that are taking place in your piece. The next list gives you some ways to do so.

1. In your writing, try to use words that say just what you want them to say.

2. Use strong, action verbs whenever you can.

   Example:
   Spencer was happy becomes *Spencer burst out laughing.*

3. Use specific nouns whenever it makes sense to do so.

   Example:
   A place becomes *a tree house.*

4. Use words that readers can see, feel, hear, smell, and taste. Some of these words are describing words or adjectives.

   Example:
   A shiny dress becomes *a glitter-covered dress.*

5. Try using a figure of speech called personification, which gives living qualities to nonliving things.

   Examples:
   • The house walked a mile to buy a coat of paint. (The house is a nonliving thing, but it's doing human-like things such as walking and buying paint.)
   • The rock cried when the wind roared.

Careful!

When you are writing a draft, your goal is to get your ideas on paper and let your thoughts flow. You are not trying to write a draft that has every detail in it, all perfectly written. Later, when you're rereading and revising your piece, you can rethink your details and decide if and how you want to improve them.

COACHING TIPS

Like a gymnast on the beam, writers perform balancing acts. One of the moves they try to balance is the way they share the details of their writing.

Writers cannot let readers see all the events that are happening in their pieces. (That would take too long and might also put their audience to sleep.) Often writers let readers see the important details, but tell them about the less important ones. If a detail is big-time important, writers do both: They let readers see it, and they also tell readers about it.

Key Points!

To balance the way you as a writer share the details in your piece, try these painless tips:

- *Important details:* Let readers see them.
- *Less important, but still needed, details:* Tell readers about them.
- *Super-important details:* Let readers see them, and tell readers about them.

Wrapping It Up!

Writers play with words and language because it's fun to do so and because they want readers to understand what they're trying to say.

One way to make the words on a page come alive for readers is to use similes or hyperboles in your writing. As long as you don't overuse them, similes and hyperboles can make your audience as happy as an elephant in a peanut factory.

Another way to grab the attention of your readers is to let them see the important details in your pieces. When writing a rough draft, you might find it easier to use telling sentences. Later, when it comes time for revising, you can experiment with language and change the telling sentences, as needed, into showing sentences.

Let's Try It!

Set #21

Sentences 1 through 5 *tell* readers what is happening or what to think. Rewrite each of them so that readers can *see* the details and decide for themselves.

Example

My teacher is nice and caring.

One possible answer: My teacher, Mr. Hart, jets out of bed early, just so that he can give students extra help before the school day starts.

Example

Bushra and her friends had a fun time at her nine-year-old birthday party.

One possible answer: On her ninth birthday, Bushra and her friends got to skate with their favorite cartoon characters at the world-famous ice show.

1. She was mad.

   _____

2. He looked tired.

   _____

3. It was pouring outside.

   _____

4. My bedroom is messy.

   _____

5. I was hungry.

_____

6. Write a story on a topic of your choice. Try to let readers see the important details that are happening. In your writing, use strong verbs, specific nouns, powerful adjectives (if needed), a simile, and a hyperbole. Share your story with a friend.

YOU ARE A CHAMPION WRITER!

Chapter 9

All Waterways Lead to Rereading and Revising

THE STARS OF THE SEA: R*E*R*E*A*D*I*N*G AND R*E*V*I*S*I*N*G

Here's a secret. Few people, if any, write perfect pieces the first, or even the second, time around—not even the author of this book. Not even Sammy, the Writing Octopus. (Shhhhhhh, don't tell!)

Good writers like you reread and revise their writing. Revising is *not* about cleaning up a shipwreck or a piece of writing that is in bad shape. The fact that you are revising a piece, rather than starting over and rewriting it, means that it is worth saving and improving. *Congratulations, Captain!*

When you revise, you are rereading your writing and making moves, such as adding or crossing out details; changing the order of sentences, choosing just-right words, and reworking the beginning or ending. Revising, then, is about making bigger changes to your writing, whereas editing is about correcting errors in capitalization, punctuation, spelling, grammar, and paragraphing.

Shhhh!

As you reread your rough draft, ask your-self questions, such as the following:

> *Where are the special parts or ideas that I might add on to and grow during revising?* (Use your captain's keen eye to spot an idea in your draft that is not only worth saving but also worth g-r-o-w-i-n-g.)

> *What parts of my writing do not work well and may confuse my readers?* (Decide whether you will revise and improve these weaker parts, or cross them out and not use them.)

The answers to these questions can give you tips for revising and improving your writing.

To help your revising efforts, try to get as many people as you can to read your piece or listen to it being read aloud. They may be able to give you ideas or suggestions for improving your writing.

Revising is not just the last stop on your writing journey: It is also every stop along the way. If you want your writing to go from good . . . to better . . . to best, try to make *rereading* and *revising* an ongoing part of your journey.

Key Points!

Like friends that bring out the best in you, the two Rs—rereading and revising—bring out the best in your writing. By re-seeing and improving your written words, you will keep your readers eager to turn the pages.

A RUBRIC THAT WON'T MAKE YOU SEASICK

The rubric or checklist below can make revising your piece of writing as painless as watching cotton candy being made at a fair.

Revising Checklist

	Yes	No
I've reread my writing many times, both silently and out loud. It makes sense and is easy to read.		
My beginning makes readers want to read on.		
My ideas tell about my topic.		
I've used interesting facts, details, and examples to develop my ideas fully.		
I've grouped like ideas together .		
My sentences begin in different ways (not *I, I, I*; not *The, The, The*).		
I am *present* in the writing. The piece sounds like I wrote it.		
I've made word choices that are *just right*.		
My ending sticks in the reader's mind; it makes readers wish my piece didn't end.		

133

PAINLESS PRACTICE

Let's take a look at a rough draft of an unfinished story, which is titled "Friends Forever." As you read the draft, think about how you might revise it.

Friends Forever

Kaitlyn is a ten-year-old girl. She has a lot of friends. Her friends' names are Candace, Kelly, and Kendall. Almost every day they play together because they are best friends. Some things they do are ride their bikes all over the neighborhood, go shopping, and play soccer. They always have fun when they hang out together. One rainy day, Kaitlyn's mom drove them to the mall in her minivan. While shopping, they had a big argument. Kaitlyn's mom had everyone return to the car. They started heading home.

I'm sure you can think of ways to improve the story. Sometimes it is easier to read and improve someone else's words, rather than our own. Yet, as authors, we must learn how to reread, rethink, and revise our own writing.

Let's talk about revising the draft, "Friends Forever." We'll begin by noticing what the author did well.

Overall, the writer did a fine job writing the rough draft. (A draft does not have to be perfect.) The author cared about the topic (friendship) and gave the reader interesting details about the kinds of things the friends in the story do while together: "ride their bikes all over the neighborhood, go shopping, and play soccer."

Here are a few suggestions (ideas) that the writer might want to think about during the revising process.

✔ Try rewriting the opening lines to make them more alive and interesting.
✔ Pay attention to word choice. Notice that the word *friends* is used three times in three sentences.
✔ Group like ideas into the same paragraph(s). When there is a change in ideas, begin a new paragraph.

There is no one right way to revise a piece of writing. In the end, it is up to the writer to decide how a piece will be revised.

Let's Try It!

Set #22

Reread and revise "Friends Forever" (page 134). Use the Revising Checklist on page 133 as a guide.

Happy Hint: Look back at the suggestions given on page 135 if you need ideas for revising the story. (Note: Many answers are possible.)

Let's sail on to the next example. As you read it, think about which one of the three paragraphs helps you, as a reader, *see* the details.

Example

Paragraph #1:

Julia has nice clothes. It's fun to go shopping with her. She always finds the cutest things to wear. Like the other day, she bought a pair of really nice jeans and boots. That's why she gets a lot of compliments about her outfits.

Paragraph #2:

Julia's clothes are as pretty as a rainbow. When we go shopping, she always looks for outfits in her favorite colors: pink and purple. Yesterday, she bought a pair of pink jeans that had violet-colored rhinestones in the shape of hearts on the back pockets. She also bought a pair of pink boots—the kind that come halfway up your calf. I'm sure she'll get a lot of compliments on her new jeans and boots.

Paragraph #3:

Julia's clothes are so pretty. I love to go shopping with her. We always stop at the pet store whenever we go to the mall. Then we go to the movies. Sometimes we even do our homework together. Julia even has the prettiest notebooks and backpack. Often they match her clothes.

Which paragraph helps you *see the details*, which in this case are the clothes? The second one, right? You can picture in your mind what the jeans looked like, with the rhinestone decorations on the back pockets; you can also imagine what the boots looked like.

Paragraph #1 gives readers the important details, but it doesn't describe them fully: "she bought a pair of really nice jeans and boots." (Readers might think that Julia bought a pair of black jeans and brown boots.)

Paragraph #3 gives readers all kinds of details, but the ones given (about the pet store, movies, and homework) do not fit the opening sentence of the paragraph: "Julia's clothes are so pretty." Good writing, then, is not about pouring just any details on the page. It's about choosing ones that are right for the piece you are writing.

By rereading and revising your words, you will make your writing clear and fun to read.

Wrapping It Up!

Writing a piece without rereading and revising it makes it as incomplete as a cupcake without frosting.

Revising is not the same as editing or proofreading. It is a way of making bigger changes to your draft—changes like adding or crossing out details, moving sentences around, and rewriting beginnings and endings.

Think of revising as a *reward*. It's your reward for doing something great—that is, for writing a terrific rough draft. So, be sure to treat yourself and your readers to that cupcake and frosting: rereading and revising.

Let's Try It!

Set #23

Reread some of your own writings. Select one piece that you want to revise, and revise it using the Revising Checklist on page 133 as a guide. Share your ideas with a friend or family member.

Chapter 10

Editing and Publishing

CLEAN UP MARINE LITTER: EDITING

Like marine litter that ruins our beautiful waters, errors can ruin a beautiful piece of writing. If you want readers to understand and enjoy your written ideas—and to believe what you have to say—take the time to edit your writing.

As a young writer, you have a brain and imagination that are as big as an ocean. From the bottom of your feet to the top of your head, you are full of amazing ideas. By revising and editing your writing, you will get your ideas and your message across to readers.

Editing is another kind of rereading. When you edit, you are rereading your writing and checking it for correctness. You are looking for and correcting errors in capitalization, punctuation, spelling, grammar, and paragraphing.

To help you spot errors in your work, reread your writing both silently (to yourself) and out loud. Writers, like you, not only *look* at what they write but also *listen* to what they write. By reading their writing aloud, writers can hear the sound of written words. They then have a better sense of what readers are seeing and hearing.

After you've edited your own writing, try asking another person like a teacher or classmate to reread and check your work.

EDITING COMPASS/CHECKLIST

When it's time to edit your piece, it helps to use a painless checklist like the one shown below.

	Yes	No
Checked my writing for neatness and correctness.		
Used capital letters correctly.		
Capitalized the first letter in proper nouns, such as names, places, and dates.		
Ended each sentence with the right punctuation (., !, or ?).		
Checked spelling.		
Underlined words that were not spelled correctly.		
Closed eyes and tried to picture how the word is spelled.		
Tried to sound the word out and look it up in the dictionary.		
Read the piece of writing backwards.		
Asked someone like a classmate for help with spelling.		
Checked grammar.		
Example: "Me and my cousin went to the movies" might become "My cousin and I went to the movies."		
Example: "A butterfly land on my windowpane" might become "A butterfly landed on my windowpane."		
Checked paragraphing.		
Indented the first line of each paragraph.		

PAINLESS PRACTICE: LETTER WRITING

It's time for an adventure in editing. Read and edit the letter below. It contains many errors in capitalization, punctuation, and spelling. Off we go on our adventure!

_____
Date

Deer Mr. Shafi,

   yesterday their was a bad smell on the back of my school bus it smelled like rotten eggs. The students on the bus held there shirts over they're nose to block in the odor.

   Eye was trying to obey the bus rules and keep my voice down. Then, the next thing I knew, Trevor and Maurice started telling the other kids that I was two blame four the smell. I wanted to cry, but I did'nt.

   Luckily, some boy named duncan told everyone to stopp teasing me. A few minutes later, Trevor and maurice told me thay were sorry.

   I want to nominate Duncan for one of your school spirit awards. He showed me kindness and helped the other kids sea that teasing is wrong.

   Tank you for being a grate principle.

                    Your Student,
                    Raphael

Now you see why it is important to edit your writing. Had Raphael sent his letter to the principal without first editing it, his message or ideas would have gotten lost in a sea of litter. Editing, then, helps to clean up the marine litter, or errors in your piece, which can come between you and your reader. Editing helps to make your writing clear and easy to read.

Take a peek at the edited copy of Raphael's letter.

_____
Date

Dear Mr. Shafi,

Yesterday there was a bad smell on the back of my school bus. **It** smelled like rotten eggs. The students on the bus held **their** shirts over **their noses** to block **out** the odor.

I was trying to obey the bus rules and keep my voice down. Then, the next thing I knew, Trevor and Maurice started telling the other kids that I was **to** blame **for** the smell. I wanted to cry, but I **didn't**.

Luckily, some boy named **Duncan** told everyone to **stop** teasing me. A few minutes later, Trevor and **Maurice** told me **they** were sorry.

I want to nominate Duncan for one of your school spirit awards. He showed me kindness and helped the other kids **see** that teasing is wrong.

Thank you for being a **great principal**.

Your Student,
Raphael

Let's Try It!
Set #24
The next letter is full of marine litter. Read it carefully and correct all errors. Use the editing checklist on page 142 as a guide.

_____
Date

Dear Mom,

I'am so mad write now. Do you know why. Last night Dad grounded me for something that was not my fault.

Hear is what happen. Melissa kept hogging the computer, even though she new it was my turn. I I my best to talk too her in a low voice, but She wouldn't listen. After an our of trying to get her unglued from the computer, I gave up trying to bee nice.

Sudenly, my face turned fire-engine read. Inn a loud, angry voice, I ordered Melissa to get of the computer. When she refused, I told her that I was going to take her clothes and toys, and give them a way.

Just then, Dad walked in. He blamed me for the hole argument. "you're the older sister; you should no better," Dad sad in a deep voice to me.

Can you belive this, Mom? I am always the won in trouble, and Melissa never gets a consequence. It's not fair.

I hop you'll talk to Dad and melissa for me. Thanks four listening.

Love
Sophia Mae

PORT OF PUBLISHING

Welcome to the Port of Publishing, Captain! It's time to publish (share or go public with) your writing. It's time to shout from the rooftops and celebrate the author in you!

There are many ways to share your published piece with an audience; you can read it aloud to other people, frame it like a photo and give it as a gift, or mail it to someone, such as a relative.

You do not have to publish everything that you write, but you should try to finish most of the pieces you start. Because you don't know how a piece will turn out until it's written, give each piece a chance to make it to home port.

A Harbor of Beginnings

Think of the Port of Publishing as a harbor of beginnings, not endings. In publishing your piece, you have done the things that writers do—observe their worlds and ask questions. Now, when you read the work of other authors, you are better able to understand the moves they're making because you're an author, too. You've returned to shore forever changed.

Congratulations Author! The poem on the next page is in honor of your seamanship and greatness.

Your Ship Has Come In: Celebrate!
by
Donna Christina Oliverio

Be proud of yourself!
Go and dance with the seals!
Have fun celebrating
how *authorship* feels!

Share your published piece
with a crew of your choice.
And let everyone hear
your writer's voice.

You've sailed a long way
from where your journey began.
You stretched your writing muscles
over and over again.

You've observed your world
with a captain's keen eye.
You spotted small ideas
and always asked why.

And just when you thought
you had reached home port,
suddenly, you realized
the piece had fallen short.

So you reread your writing
and revised it some more.
Cleaned up all marine litter.
And have arrived safely at shore.

Now that it's done,
you're amazed to find.
You have other writing ideas
already in mind.

Throw your cap in the air, Captain!
Your ship has come in!
Welcome to the port
of publishing!

It's a harbor of beginnings
as you shall find.
It's a whole new world
Now that you have a writer's mind.

Answer Key

CHAPTER I

Answers to Let's Try It! Set #1
Many answers are possible. Here are some.

1. My brother hogging the computer, when he knows that it's my turn
2. Thank-you note to Uncle Billy and Aunt Tillie for buying me the remote control race car
3. Newspaper story or magazine article about the best and worst toys for kids
4. Send e-mail to friends about the birthday party I'm having at the amusement park
5. Poems about the moon and sun
6. How to books: how to play soccer and how to play a musical instrument
7. Journal entry: my search for missing treasure
8. Use fun facts about animals to make up riddles **Example:** What kind of fish has a face that looks like a horse's face and a tail that can wrap around your finger like a monkey's tail? (Riddle Answer: A sea-horse, of course.)

Answers to Let's Try It! Set #2
1. Reread the two plays in the chapter (pages 3–5 and 8–11). Underline the main (big) ideas or points. Many answers are possible. Compare your answers with a friend.
2. Here are some possible answers.
   • Writing is like playing a video game. You become better with practice.
   • Read and write as much as you can. Other writers can give you ideas for improving your own pieces.
   • Ideas for writing are everywhere.

3. Have fun acting out the play! If you perform the play in front of an audience, speak clearly and make sure that your listeners can hear you.

CHAPTER 2

Answers to Let's Try It! Set #3

1. Many answers are possible. Here are two sample answers.

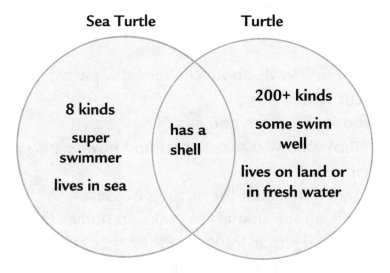

Sea Turtle / Turtle

8 kinds
super swimmer
lives in sea

has a shell

200+ kinds
some swim well
lives on land or in fresh water

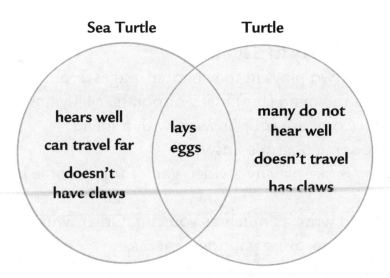

Sea Turtle / Turtle

hears well
can travel far
doesn't have claws

lays eggs

many do not hear well
doesn't travel
has claws

Happy Hint: Writers like you are always thinking, asking why, and trying to figure out things. When they read, for example, that a sea turtle cannot pull inside its shell, they might wonder, "How does the creature protect itself?" Or, when they learn that a sea turtle has flippers, they figure out on their own that the creature is an excellent swimmer.

CHAPTER 3

Answers to Let's Try It! Set #4

Many answers are possible. Enjoy the freedom that a rough draft gives you. Get your thoughts down on paper as well as you can.

The sample outline on pages 25–26 gives you an idea of how to set up your rough draft. Try rereading Chapter 2 and/or doing more research if you need more information.

Answers to Let's Try It! Set #5

Many answers are possible. If you get stuck, reread the poems in the chapter or ones written by your favorite poets.

CHAPTER 4

Answers to Let's Try It! Set #6

1. Eating Celery—No
   If you as a reader came across the title "Eating Celery," would you find it exciting or catchy? Probably not, right? Also, although Jay Jay does eat celery while waiting for Miss Wheels and his mom to finish talking, his doing so is only a small event in the story.
2. It's a Bird . . . It's a Plane . . . It's a Roller-Skating Rabbit!—Yes. This title matches the story and gets the reader's attention.
3. Carrot Shakes—No
   Miss Wheels and Jay Jay do sip carrot shakes at the fair. However, carrot shakes make up only a small part of the story.

4. Miss Wheels Teaches a Special Rabbit How to Roller Skate—Yes
   This title matches the story, but it is not exciting.
5. Skating Through Sadness into Gladness—Yes
6. There are many possible answers.

Answers to Let's Try It! Set #7

Many answers are possible. Here is one possible answer:

In "Jay Jay, the Roller-Skating Rabbit," the main characters are Jay Jay and Miss Wheels. Jay Jay is a grayish-brown rabbit who has never been able to hop. Miss Wheels is Jay Jay's babysitter and also a roller-skating coach.

Jay Jay's character changes over time. He spends much of his childhood feeling "down in the dumps," because he can't hop around like other bunnies. Then, when he meets Miss Wheels, Jay Jay becomes more hopeful. At times, Jay Jay is funny. He talks about the flops he took when he was first learning to roller skate, as well as the multiskater pile-up he got caught in the middle of.

Miss Wheels wants the best for Jay Jay. She is caring and does kind things for him, like brushing his fur daily and making his favorite dessert, spinach pudding. She also gives Jay Jay excellent advice about safety.

Miss Wheels wears colorful clothing and fun jewelry, like pink and white polka dot shorts and a bracelet with roller-skating charms on it. The way she dresses matches the fact that she's a roller-skating coach and also a babysitter.

With the help of Miss Wheels, Jay Jay decides to let go of his sadness. He trains hard and learns to roller skate. He doesn't become the world's best roller skater, but he always does his best and wins a trophy known as the Carrot Cup. For Jay Jay, roller skating is more than just a sport. It is the means he uses to move about.

Answers to Let's Try It! Set #8

In "Jay Jay, the Roller-Skating Rabbit," the conflict is that Jay Jay is a rabbit who, ever since birth, has been unable to hop. His problem sets the whole story in motion, beginning with the sadness he feels because he cannot hop and continuing with his struggles to learn to roller skate.

Answers to Let's Try It! Set #9

1. Many answers are possible. Ask a friend or relative to listen to your story and give you suggestions.
2. Many answers are possible. The chart and sample answers give you some ideas.

Reasons for Setting a Wild Animal Free	Reasons for Keeping a Wild Animal as a Pet
An animal that is born in the wild belongs in the wild; it will be unhappy if it is kept as a pet.	The animal doesn't have to worry about food and shelter.
Some people keep a wild animal for the wrong reasons; they may, for example, force the animal to learn difficult tricks or moves, like water-skiing—and then try to make money off the animal's talents.	The animal doesn't have to worry about protecting itself from wild predators.
Even if the animal grows to love its owner, it will never get over the pain of not returning to its home in the wild.	The animal will get used to its owner and feel safe.
	Overall, the animal's life will be easier, because the owner will do almost everything for it.

Sample Answer: Reasons for Setting a Wild Animal Free

It is wrong to keep a wild animal as a pet. A wild animal belongs in the wild. Nature is its home.

A wild animal that is forced to live in someone's home or yard will become sad, sickened, and confused. It may stop drinking and eating. The poor animal will not understand why it has been removed from the only environment it has ever known—the beautiful wilderness.

Some pet owners make money off the animals that are in their care. They may, for example, train animals to perform difficult tricks in front of large crowds. Imagine how frightened an animal such as a squirrel would feel if it is forced to learn to water-ski.

Wild animals must be set free! They will not be happy or healthy if they are kept as pets.

Sample Answer: Reasons for Keeping a Wild Animal as a Pet

There are many reasons for owning a wild animal.

One reason is that the animal will not have to hunt or find shelter. Its owner will make sure that it has plenty of food and a loving home. The new environment will be much safer than the wilderness. In time the owner and animal will become best friends.

Another good reason for keeping a wild animal as a pet is if the animal is either sick or hurt. An injured animal, such as a rabbit that has been hit by a car, will have a hard time surviving in the wild. By caring for the injured animal, and by not setting it free, caring pet owners can nurse it back to health. They can protect the animal from predators and other dangers, like extra cold winters or hurricanes.

A good owner makes sure that an animal is happy and safe. As long as someone is a loving owner, there is nothing wrong with that person keeping a wild animal as a pet. The animal will have no worries and will feel as if it's on vacation.

CHAPTER 5

Answers to Let's Try It! Set #10
Many answers are possible. Here are sample answers.

- Begin with action. *As Ben ran full-speed toward the finish line, he could feel Carl closing in behind him.* Note: You can rewrite the sentence about Ben (the sample answer) in different ways. Here is one: *Ben ran full-speed toward the finish line. His family and friends cheered him on. Suddenly, their cheers turned to silence. Another runner was closing in behind him.*
- Open with dialogue or conversation. *"Don't play ball in the house!" said Mom to her three-year-old daughter, Payton.*
- Start off with a sound effect. *Bang! Crash! Splat! Jodi dropped her brand-new pair of eyeglasses on the kitchen tile.*
- Begin with a surprising question. *If birds eat more than twice their weight in food, why do people say "You eat like a bird" to people who do not eat a lot?*
- Begin with a surprising sentence. *I would rather take out the garbage than play a video game.*
- Introduce an interesting character. *Igor, the Spotted Owl, only comes out at night. He has night vision, which allows him to see in the dark while hunting field mice.*

Answers to Let's Try It! Set #11
Answers will vary. Many answers are possible.

CHAPTER 6

Answers to Let's Try It! Set #12

1. Reread the fairy tale. Many answers are possible. Here is a sample answer.

The fairy tale taught me that good writers choose their words carefully. If I want readers to care about my writing, then I must care about it. One way to show readers that I care is to use words that are exciting and that fit the piece I am writing.

In the beginning of the fairy tale, a book full of boring words is sad and lonely. Young fish (children) do not check it out of the underwater library. Its pages are dull; they make young fish snooze.

The problem in the fairy tale was solved when King Sammy helped the author revise the dull words in the book. Once the book was revised, young fish wanted to stay up past their bedtimes to read it.

How will I keep my readers from falling asleep? I'll think about them the whole time that I'm writing and use words that will keep them eager to turn the pages. I'll also use words that say just what I want them to say. Luckily, there are a gazillion words in our language for me to choose from.

2. Many answers are possible.

Answers to Let's Try It! Set #13

Reread your paragraph and make sure that it describes the horse in the picture. Have a friend or family member read your paragraph and give you suggestions.

Many answers are possible. Here is one:

A beautiful horse, standing in the middle of a field, cranes its neck to sniff the ground. She presses her face into the grainy texture of the dirt. Suddenly, the crisp grass tickles her nose and makes her hungry. I hear a chomping sound as she eats the healthy vegetation. Watching this animal makes me realize that this is her grazing land. The field belongs to her.

Answers to Let's Try It! Set #14

Have your classmates or family members read your description and see if they can figure out which blanket you are describing.
Many answers are possible. Here are two sample answers.

Sample Answer for Blanket A: My horse, Freedom, is a clothes horse. She always nudges me to buy her fancy hats and blankets. Her new blanket has two vertical lines that are separated by a horizontal line. It has two suns, one in the bottom left corner and one in the top right corner. There is a star in the bottom right corner. A crescent moon sits between the star and one of the suns. Freedom is the best dressed horse in my town.

Sample Answer for Blanket C: I bought a straw hat and blanket for my horse, Bernard. On the left side of the blanket, there are two suns, one on top of the other. On the right side, there are two stars, also one on top of the other. In the middle, toward the bottom, is a crescent moon. I'm so proud of the way Bernard looks in his new clothes. And, judging by the way he stands and walks around, so is he!

Answers to Let's Try It! Set #15

Many answers are possible. If your answer is not listed below, you can check it either by looking it up in a dictionary or thesaurus, or by asking someone to help you.

Sad—gloomy, depressed, dismal
Big—gigantic, enormous, large, huge, vast
Little—tiny, petite, modest
Nice—pleasant, kind, polite, fine
Great—grand, vast, huge
Good—superior, excellent, fine
Bad—terrible, awful, horrible, unpleasant
Hot—burning, scorching, sizzling, warm, boiling
Mad—angry, furious, annoyed
Old—aged, mature, ancient
Scared—frightened, afraid, terrified, fearful, nervous, timid

CHAPTER 7

Answers to Let's Try It! Set #16

Notice that there are many possible answers.

1. Weak Verb: The first baseman hit the ball over the fence in left field.
   Strong Verb: The first baseman hammered (slammed, smashed, or cracked) the ball over the fence in left field.
2. Weak Verb: Avery is holding the baseball.
   Strong Verb: Avery is gripping (grasping, clutching) the baseball.
3. Weak Verb: Ned, Sam, and Joshua left the field.
   Strong Verb: Ned, Sam, and Joshua dashed (darted, hurried, skipped) off the field.
4. Weak Verb: Ariel and Caroline were happy when their team won.
   Strong Verb: Ariel and Caroline jumped for joy (exploded with delight) when their team won.

5. Weak Verb: Leaves <u>fell</u> onto the playing field.
   Strong Verb: Leaves <u>blew</u> (<u>floated</u>, <u>soared</u>) onto the playing field.
6. Weak Verb: Jonathan <u>ate</u> a hot dog and French fries at the baseball game.
   Strong Verb: Jonathan <u>devoured</u> (<u>gulped</u> down, <u>inhaled</u>) a hot dog and French fries at the baseball game.
7. There are many possible answers.

Answers to Let's Try It! Set #17

1. There are many possible answer choices. Here is one.

   Smack in the middle of an exciting football game, a **cocker spaniel** began chasing the **quarterback**. **Marion** and **Tom** could not believe their eyes. The animal tried to tug at the player's **helmet** and **cleats**. Luckily, **a family with two small children** came along carrying a huge bag of **popcorn**. The food distracted the dog, and he left the player alone. The **fans**, **cheerleaders**, and even the **referee** roared.

2. Answers will vary.

Answers to Let's Try It! Set #18

1. The weak verb that was used is *got*, as in "She got the ball."
2. *Got* is a weak verb because it doesn't show readers how the action happened or how something was received.
3. Three other adjectives, or describing words, for ball are *colorful*, *plastic*, and *bouncing*. (There are many possible answers here.)
4. The strong verb that was used is *grabbed*. The sentence "Darla grabbed the basketball" shows readers how the action happened and, also, how the action did not happen. Darla reached for, took, or stole the ball; she did not get or receive it by chance.
5. The two specific nouns used were *Darla* (a proper noun) and *basketball*. They add more information to the general nouns "she" and "ball."

CHAPTER 8

Answers to Let's Try It! Set #19

Many answers are possible. Here are sample answers.

1. Sarah's fingernail is as short as an ant's leg.
2. Mr. Nelson is as funny as a monkey on roller skates.
3. Writing is like building a tree house; the words are the pieces of wood and building blocks you use to create a story.
4. Felicia is as sweet as a truckload of sugar cubes.
5. Writing a paper without revising it is like trying to fly a kite with a short string; you can do it but you won't get very far.
6. The answers depend on the songs and poems you choose.
7. The answers depend on the pictures you cut out from magazines or newspapers.
8. "Revising is Sammy's close friend" is not a simile. Similes do not say that one thing is another; they say that one thing is *like* another. "Revising is Sammy's close friend" is a metaphor. Metaphors say that one thing (revising) *is* another (Sammy's close friend).

Answers to Let's Try It! Set #20

Many answers are possible. Here are sample answers.

1. It was so hot out today that the potato plants turned into French fries.
2. Michelle has so many books in her house that you need a card catalog to find the one you want.
3. Omar is such an awesome basketball player that he can make a basket even when he is three miles away from the hoop.
4. It is so cold outside that even the polar bears need blankets.
5. Tara's eyelashes are so long that when she blinks, she cools the room off better than an air conditioner.
6. Her teeth sparkle so much that whenever she smiles, people run to get their sunglasses.

7. Answers will vary.
8. Answers will vary.

Answers to Let's Try It! Set #21
Answers will vary. Here are sample answers.

1. She slammed the door, growled at her brother, and stomped her feet.
2. His eyes were set back, with dark circles under them.
3. I put on my raincoat, opened my umbrella, and raced to my neighbor's house—dodging the many puddles along the way.
4. I am forced to do a balancing act when I enter my bedroom because there are dirty clothes and crumbled papers scattered all over the place.
5. I devoured two bowls of cereal, an egg sandwich, and an energy bar all in one sitting.

CHAPTER 9

Answers to Let's Try It! Set #22
Here is one way to revise "Friends Forever." Notice that the title has been revised.

Friends Forever, or Enemies Everlasting?

If you're like ten-year-old Kaitlyn, you think that friends are the scoops of ice cream on the cone of life.

When Kaitlyn hangs out with her three best friends—Candace, Kelly, and Kendall—they always have more fun than a sloth hanging upside down from a tree. They enjoy riding their bikes all over their neighborhood, going shopping, talking on the telephone, and playing soccer.

One rainy day, Kaitlyn's mom drove the four girls to the mall in her minivan. While shopping, they had such a huge argument that Kaitlyn's mom ordered everyone to get back in the van. And, off for home they headed.

The revised title, "Friends Forever, or Enemies Everlasting?" makes readers wonder what will happen in the story. They read on to find out.

Notice the first sentence of the revised story: "If you're like ten-year-old Kaitlyn, you think that friends are the scoops of ice cream on the cone of life." The sentence is not a show stopper, but it is more exciting than the one in the rough draft: "Kaitlyn is a ten-year-old girl."

The writer uses interesting language to describe the fun the girls have: "They always have more fun than a sloth hanging upside down from a tree."

Rather than repeat the word *friends*, the writer plays with the order of sentences and also with words. (The word *girls* replaces *friends* in one sentence.)

Ideas that are alike are grouped into paragraphs.

Answers to Let's Try It! Set #23
1. Answers will vary. Ask someone like a friend or teacher to check your work.

CHAPTER 10

Answers to Let's Try It! Set #24

————————
                                         Date

Dear Mom,

    I **am** (or **I'm**) so mad **right** now. Do you know why**?** Last night Dad grounded me for something that was not my fault.

    Here is what **happened**. Melissa kept hogging the computer, even though she **knew** it was my turn. I **tried** my best to talk **to** her in a low voice, but **she** wouldn't listen. After an **hour** of trying to get her unglued from the computer, I gave up trying to **be** nice.

    Suddenly, my face turned fire-engine **red**. **In** a loud, angry voice, I ordered Melissa to get **off** the computer. When she refused, I told her that I was going to take her clothes and toys, and give them **away**.

    Just then, Dad walked in. He blamed me for the **whole** argument. "**You're** the older sister; you should **know** better," Dad **said** in a deep voice to me.

    Can you **believe** this, Mom? I am always the **one** in trouble, and Melissa never gets a consequence. It's not fair.

    I **hope** you'll talk to Dad and **Melissa** for me. Thanks **for** listening.

                           Love,
                           Sophia Mae

Index